YPRES

THE HOLY GROUND
OF BRITISH ARMS

PLAN OF YPRES.

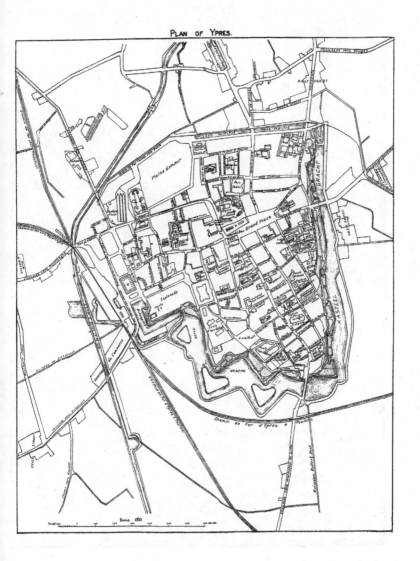

1 Le Palais des Seigneurs.
2 St. Martin.
3 St. Nicolas.
4 St. François.

5 L'Hôpital.
6 De Katte.
7 De boterpoorte.
8 St. Pierre.

9 De tempelpoorte
10 Les cordeliers.
11 De Roo
12 St. Dominique.

13 La maison d'insensez.
14 L'Hôpital de S. Jean
15 De Boesing poorte
16 St. Jacques.

17 Le marché
18 De torre poorte.
19 St Jean.
20 De blende poorte

DURING THE BATTLES OF YPRES

LIEUT.-COLONEL BECKLES WILLSON

Y P R E S

THE HOLY GROUND
OF BRITISH ARMS

The Naval & Military Press Ltd

Published by

The Naval & Military Press Ltd

Unit 5 Riverside, Brambleside
Bellbrook Industrial Estate
Uckfield, East Sussex
TN22 1QQ England

Tel: +44 (0)1825 749494

www.naval–military–press.com
www.nmarchive.com

CONTENTS

YPRES — PANORAMA

PUBLISHER'S PREFACE

In 1916, after nearly two years of fighting, there was an agitation in political and military circles both in London and Paris to " straighten out the Ypres Salient " (as the phrase went) i. e. to withdraw the British line so that it would run north and south through or behind the town. Had this agitation succeeded, the result would have been disastrous for the tiny Strip of Belgium which alone remained to represent the Kingdom of His Majesty, King Albert I.

Amongst those who most vigorously opposed this proposal was the author of this Handbook. For a time he experienced great difficulty in obtaining permission to express his views, but at length, sanction was obtained from the War Office, and in August 1916 the little volume " In the Ypres Salient, " previously issued privately and distributed amongst the Canadian Corps, was published.

The volume ostensibly related the story of the Canadian fighting in the Salient : but its real purpose was to persuade the British public of the necessity for holding that tract of territory, in spite of all arguments to the contrary.

The book made a deep and widespread impression. Recognising its value as propaganda the British Foreign Office ordered a gratis special large edition to be printed and distributed. There is no doubt that Colonel Beckles Willson's eloquent arguments went far to convince public opinion that Ypres and the Salient must be defended from motives of high policy.

The Publisher desires, therefore to preface this Handbook with the following extract from the authors book " In the Ypres Salient " published in 1916. *

* *In the Ypres Salient :* Simpkin, Marshall and Co. Ltd. London.

" It is said that Ypres and the Salient are chiefly retained for sentimental reasons. This is true, in the sense that this whole war was avowedly waged, in the first instance for sentimental reasons.

Not long ago, a French General said to me that the Germans were attacking Verdun, and the French were defending it, not for strategical but for political and dynastic reasons. " If they took Verdun to-morrow, they could not advance, but to lose Verdun would be for France a blow over the heart. "

When we pledged our honour to Belgium, we were pledged to the hilt to guard the soil of Ypres inviolate from the heel of the living enemy. It is only a heap of ruins, but it is an eternal memorial of British valour. It is only a shellswept graveyard, but the graves are those of our heroic dead.

To abandon Ypres now would tarnish our banners. It would be like offering our sister for violation because she had been bruised and buffeted with stones.

Military strategy very properly takes into account political and moral prestige, and to " straighten out the Salient " by the voluntary abandonment of a single mile of ground would inflict upon us a moral and political loss equal to an Army corps. If Ypres goes, Belgium goes, and if Belgium goes, whatever the final issue, something of glory passes from the allied arms.

It is a terrible responsibility to stand steadfast but every soldier who has died in the Ypres Salient has yielded his life to protect his country's honour. Vulnerable the Salient may be, but our troops are invulnerable. While they continue so, Ypres and this little remaining fragment of Belgian soil and the path to Calais are safe. "

BRUGES
January 3rd 1920

x

AUTHOR'S FOREWORD

In a short time tens of thousands of Englishmen and women will be making a pilgrimage to the battlefields of France and Flanders. To those who visit Ypres and desire to learn something of the history of this famous town as well as an account of the chief battles during four years in one comparatively small patch of country, I offer this little book.

During its past history Ypres has been Flemish, Spanish, French, Dutch and Belgian; but no matter what flag flies or whether it arises from its ruins, it must be forever British. Almost Every soldier in the British Army has fought at Ypres; a quarter of a million are sleeping their eternal sleep there. Every soldier treasures memories of Ypres. In Italy, I was asked about Ypres. I found men of the Welsh Fusiliers in Egypt who wanted to know if Goldfisch Chateau had been hit yet and if the bridge over the Lille Gate had gone; and when I rode into Damascus, I recognised an officer whom I had last seen by the Ypres Canal Bank. We lunched together and exchanged Ypres gossip for an hour.

For centuries to come they will be digging British bones and British cartridges out of the soil of the Salient. The enemy suffered even more terribly there : but it was a defeat for him and the honour and glory of the defence was ours : for the victory was ours. On the maps the reader will not find the homely nomenclature of the war.

As our troops got familiar with the topography of the Salient a good many familiar names began to spring into history. Of course, there were many Picadilly Circuses and Strands. One of the earliest was " Shell trap Farm ", on the St. Julien road which was a good name, as it exactly indicated the terrific receptacle it became for enemy shells; but somebody at headquarters thought it conveyed an idea of the success of his " frightfulness " to the Boche; so the name was changed to " Mouse Trap Farm ". Then we had " Hell Fire Corner ", where the Roulers railway cross the Menin road; " Clapham Junction " the high ground on the same road past Hooghe and " Salvation Corner " just north of the town on the Boesinghe road.

Many officers and men entertain vivid memories of Canal Bank just north of Ypres. The dugouts there which were the headquarters for so many British brigades, were on the east side of the canal, and were formerly a row of small farm-houses. As time went on, the units stationed there employed material, bricks and timber, and constructed homes of quite a durable and respectable character. These dugouts, which were dignified by resounding names, were the scenes of much that was memorable in the war, the planning of attacks, visits of notable commanders, return of wounded heroes, many glorious mess jollifications, so that legends grew up about them, and the officers and men who had been billetted there at different periods during the war, found in recalling them a bond of unity. After the Armistice, they continued very much as they had been during the war. I made numerous efforts to save them as historical souvenirs, but my efforts were too late, and the dugouts fell a prey to the German prisoners employed in salvage operations.

In spite of the protests of right-thinking Belgians, as well as of ourselves, a small clique was determined to turn Ypres' war celebrity into commercial profit. It was not even as if these inn-keepers and dramsellers came from Ypres: a large proportion belonged elsewhere, from Brussels and the towns in German occupation. Many of the cabarets are run by prosperous entrepreneurs elsewhere, as a sort of Ypres branch of their business.

The whole place took on the aspect of a cheap holiday resort or country fair and so, unless the Belgian Government takes action, it will remain.

It has, however, finally been decided by an Anglo-Belgian Commission to leave the Cloth Hall and Cathedral ruins untouched. But the enclosure was arranged hastily and the approaches to these ruins are miserably insufficient. If the erection of restaurants and estaminets continues in the Grand' Place in a short time it will be difficult on account of their ignoble environment, even to see the beautiful thirteenth century vestiges which would have commanded the interest, admiration and reverence of the whole civilized world.

Ypres should be the one great and sacred repository of all the scattered dead in the Salient.

No more fitting or nobler cemetery could there be on earth for those dead youths who now lie out in the mud and mist of the Flanders fields. What a fitting setting would be these shattered churches and convent walls-enclosing smooth English green sward! A great marble chapel and sanctuary should be built opposite the Cloth Hall in the Grand' Place. Each Division in the British Army could have its own spacious plot — the Guards in the shadow of St. Jacques — the troops who stemmed the tide in October, 1914, overlooked by the high, ancient fragment of St. Peters. The cemeteries of the first Seven Divisions would range along the streets by the eastern Menin Gate whose cobblestones are worn by the tramp during those four years of our infantry and the restless wheels of our guns.

There is not a single half-acre in Ypres that is not sacred. There is not a stone which has not sheltered scores of loyal young hearts, whose one impulse and desire was to fight and if need be, to die for England. Their blood has drenched its cloisters and its cellars, but if never a drop had been spilt, if never a life had been lost in the defence of Ypres still would Ypres be hallowed, if only for the hopes and the courage it has inspired and the scenes of valour and sacrifice it has witnessed. MENIN GATE.

YPRES.

November 16th 1919.

XIII

YPRES

ITS HISTORY

Can we evoke the past glory of YPRES ? Can we reconstruct for the eager eye of the mind those churches and convents, public edifices and beautiful shops and dwellings which once compelled the admiration of the traveller, the artist and the scholar ? Can we again behold the ancient warriors and burghers who in the far off Middle ages flocked about the streets and ramparts, busy with war and commerce, proud of their beautiful city, a city of 200.000 souls, whose fame spread through the length and breadth of Europe ?

Yes, one could doubtless do all this did one but possess learning enough and imagination enough, even as Lord Macaulay boasted that he could in fancy conjure up the architecture and the street scenes of the 17th. century as he took his daily stroll down Whitehall. But such a re-creative faculty is rare even in the most devoted tourist ; and to-day in the case of Ypres the difficulty has been terribly enhanced by the mighty four years tempest of war which broke over the ancient town and, departing, left it almost levelled to the earth in shapeless and desolate ruin.

Yet what Ypres has lost of its architectural wealth and beauty, what has vanished of its ancient memorials and its people, it has gained in the priceless symbolism conferred upon it by the Great War. No fire or steel or poison-fumes can rob it of its new glory in the annals of the British Empire. It is in the words of the soldier-poet, Rupert Brooke, " a corner of a foreign land that is forever England."

What Jerusalem is to the Jewish race, what Mecca

is to the Mohamedan, Ypres must always be to the millions who have in that long conflict lost a husband, son or brother, slain in its defence and who sleep their eternal sleep within sight of its silent belfry. Ypres and the expanse of earth spread out eastward is in truth the " Holy Ground of British Arms." For the tens of thousands of gallant Frenchmen who fought and fell here it must also be sacred to our Allies. One should note that to the Germans also Ypres is deemed sacred. In the official German account of the 1914 campaign issued by the German General Staff is the passage : " The battle of Ypres will be a memorial to German heroism and self sacrifice for all time and will long remain a source of inspiration for the historian and the poet " * But the brunt of the defence for four years fell upon us and 250,000 British dead lie within its borders.

According to the ancient Latin Chronicle Ypres other-wise *Hypra* derives its name from Hyperborus, a " certain
HYPRA FOUNDED captain of ancient Britain, to-day called England ". ** This warrior first established himself, we are told, with 700 German slaves at the place to-day called LANGEMARCK — an astonishing anticipation of recent war history. The first authentic record, of the town however does not begin until the year A. D. 960 when Ypres is described as consisting of a few houses grouped about a small castle in an island of the Yperlea in front of the site of the present gateway to the ancient St. Martin's Close.

So rapid was its growth that as early as 1073 it was an important village with two widely separated parish churches, drawing its wealth from cloth-weaving and enjoying royal liberties and municipal privileges.

To the Counts of Flanders was largely due its rapid growth and prosperity so that Yper (or Ypres) became in the

* *Die Schlacht... bei Ypern im Herbst, 1914.*
** Quoted by Guicciardini I. *Paese Bassi* 1568.

twelfth and thirteenth centuries the metropolis of Flanders, greater and more important than either Bruges or Ghent. In 1267, as we learn from a petition to Pope Innocent IV, the aldermen estimated its population at 200,000 souls. It boasted 4000 looms and seven parish churches and was by the aid of the Draper's Guild able to build the vast Draper's Guild Hall (called by us the Cloth Hall) the largest and most beautiful secular monument of the Middle ages in all Flanders. Ypres had also a mint of its own. Its aldermen (échevins) exercised supreme judiciary power. Merchants from all parts of Europe flocked hither and had their counting houses here, and the sovereigns of France and England as well as the Emperor of Germany granted privileges to the men of Ypres who came to trade within their realms.

But not many centuries was all this wealth and prosperity to endure. Its freedom and privileges were assailed in the fourteenth century by its former patrons. The Counts of Flanders and Ypres were driven to enter into a defensive alliance with Bruges and Ghent resulting in sanguinary wars which were waged also against the Kings of England and of France, the latter " ever hostile to the Flemish nation ". Thus on June 9th. 1383, the city was besieged by English troops of Richard II under the warlike Bishop of Norwich assisted by a body of Ghent Burghers who were commercially rivals of Ypres. The fierceness of the fighting is described by contemporary chroniclers, one of whom declares that " in one day were picked up in the streets of Ypres so many arrows as to fill over-full two tuns. " When however, Charles VI, King of France, came to the relief of his beleaguered fortress of Ypres, the Gantois and the terrible English bowmen promptly retired. The siege had lasted until August 10th. The whole of the suburbs were destroyed, together with thousands of looms, so that a general exodus of weavers began. The cloth trade declined and the foreign

2

traders, weary of the incessant and bloody civil wars left the city. In addition came the horrors of the Great Plague. Ypres, at the beginning of the fifteenth century had ceased to be the commercial metropolis of Flanders although 100.000 inhabitants still dwelt within its walls.

Then came the era of the Dukes of Burgundy, when Ypres was engaged in a struggle to maintain such freedom and commerce as it still possessed. It could not arrest the decay; but for a century or two it kept its place as the third of the cities of Flanders. Under Phillip II it was created a bishopric. In the great religious wars which soon broke out, it became the victim of the iconoclastic fury of the Protestant fanatics. The whole of the province became **PILLAGES &** involved in pillage and massacre. Reaction **MASSACRES** ensued and the Spanish soldiers of Alva continued the destruction. Ypres was captured and sacked by the Gueux (1578) and by Alexander Farnese six years later. Gradually the industrious weavers, who had made the cloth of Ypres (d'Yper, from whence our word *diaper*) celebrated throughout Europe, sick of the many sieges, and the turmoil and bloodshed, deserted the city, fleeing to England and Holland in their tens of thousands. At the end of that century it is said only 5000 inhabitants remained in Ypres. Most of the town was in ruins.

During the seventeenth century Ypres was four times captured by the French — and indeed it only figures in the history of that era as the scene of sieges, bombardments and capitulations, with pillage and ruinous taxation in their train. It remained in the possession of the French until 1715.

Thus was Ypres for more than two centuries the sport of historic misfortunes. At the time of the French revolution it fell into the hands of the troops of the Convention and, says a local chronicler, writing on the eve of the Great War " for the last time our town became the scene of violence and destruction. "

The French Revolutionary Convention imposed upon Ypres a system of political and religious repression. Its municipal independance, preserved so jealously for six centuries and throughout so many disasters, was revoked and in 1801, as a result of the Concordat, the Episcopal See of Ypres, once filled by the famous Bishop Cornelius Janssen, (founder of the Janssenist sect) was suppressed.

Afterwards came the Dutch ascendency, when the fortifications rebuilt by the great French engineer Vauban were restored and extended. But when the Belgian kingdom was established, in order to remove the fears and susceptibilities of Napoleon III, its Government ordered the fortress to be dismantled and the ramparts were converted into peaceful promenades.

At the outbreak of the Great War Ypres was a quiet picturesque town of some 18.000 inhabitants, revealing in its noble Cloth Hall, stately churches and its many charitable institutions striking evidence of its former pride and prosperity.

A DESCRIPTION OF

YPRES

CLOTH HALL The imposing ruins which dominate the extensive Grand' Place are those of the most notable building of its kind in Belgium, the world-famous Cloth Hall or Draper's Guildhall, of whose bulk only half a wall, a fragment of the Belfry remains.

This building (or group of buildings) comprised the Cloth Hall proper, the Belfry, the Nieuwerck, the Salle des Echevins (or Aldermen's Council Chamber), the Town Hall and the Hall of the Council of Twenty-seven. To the whole group is given locally the name of *Les Halles*.

The first stone of the Belfry which was the centre of the Cloth Hall, was laid March 1. 1201 by Baldwin IX, Count of Flanders and Emperor of Constantinople. The east wing was completed in 1230. The western and northern portions of the Hall date from 1285 and the whole building was finished in 1304. This vast structure was used by the Drapers Guild as their warehouse and exchange, with offices for the inventory and despatch of goods. It was a striking example of early Gothic. The three façades had three stories each, flanked by corner turrets. In the niches of the top-story were statues of the Counts of Flanders and illustrious Yprians. These were destroyed by the French in 1793, being replaced in 1854-1875. The building extended on both sides of the Belfry, with a frontage of 433 feet. On the ground floor were a series of rectangular doorways, surmounted by a quat-

YPRES — THE HALLES

refoil. The whole building was covered by a lofty slate roof, along the top of which ran a crest of stonework. The ground floor of the Hall was latterly used for various public purposes, such as the police station, municipal weigh-house, and a vegetable, flower, and butter market. The brickwork vaulting was supported by short massive stone pillars, save in the north wing, where the ancient wooden floor of the upper room rested on a row of ten straight circular columns.

In the centre of the main façade rose the great square belfry, 230 feet high, with turrets at the angles.

To the eastern extremity of the Cloth Hall was added in 1620-24 a graceful Renaissance structure in yellowish stone. This came to occupy the site of various temporary wooden buildings, to which the name Nieuwerck (New Work) had been given, and the old name was inherited by the new building. It possessed a beauty and lightness which made the beholder overlook the want of harmony with the greater edifice. Its groundfloor consisted of an elegant open hall, twenty feet wide, boldly supported on columns, with carved capitals and firmly bound by girders. North and south the roof ended in graceful gables; there were numerous windows in the roof. The Nieuwerck was 105 feet in length.

Up to 1794 this building was used by the Aldermen of Ypres, who had also their private chapel there, of which the east window remained a relic until the 1914 bombardment.

To enter the Cloth Hall, the visitor passed under the vaulted basement of the Nieuwerck and turning to the left entered the Town Hall (Hotel de Ville) which is on the north side, opposite St. Martin's church. It occupied the site of a fourteenth century Stedehaus, which was destroyed by fire in 1498. This structure was then hastily built out of the old materials, which accounted for the shortcomings of its architecture in comparison with the adjoining edifice. Through the Town Hall the visitor ascended a great stair-

YPRES — TOWNHALL

case, flanked by great paintings, leading to the Great Hall.
Inside the Nieuwerck, it may be mentioned in passing, was
situated the Burgomaster's room, a small chamber richly
wainscotted, containing a fine picture of the Grand' Place in
the last century.   It was to this room that the German invad-
ing commander came on October 7th to issue his edict to the
burgomaster, M. Colaert, who was held hostage, together
with several of the aldermen, for the payment of the sum of
70,000 francs, all the money in the treasury.   One of the
other rooms was the Blue room, containing several paintings,
and the Throne Room, in the Empire style, also containing
pictures.   Other rooms housed the extensive and valuable
archives of Ypres, including the ancient charters, deposit-
ed in a splendid 15th century oak chest.

Passing through a covered gallery, dating from 1551 one
entered the Great Hall, which occupied the whole of the
first floor of the Cloth Hall.   The open timber roof lent a

THE GREAT HALL   fine effect to the interior, the oak being
very massive.   Between the supports were
a series of mural paintings on a large scale
commemorating the past history of Ypres.
These were the work of Ferdinand Pauwels and Louis Delbeke of Ypres, and from these two painters the two parts
of the Great Hall took their name, being known respectively
as the Salle Pauwels and the Salle Delbeke.   The effect produced by the pictures of the Salle Pauwels was most striking,
the subjects beginning with the Visit of Count Philip of
Alsace to the Hospital of our Lady in 1187 and ending with
an Episode in the Siege of Ypres by the English and men
of Ghent in 1383.   One of them was entitled : " the Return
of the Armed Forces of Ypres after the Battle of the Golden
Spurs ". Another bore the title: " Count Ferdinand of Port-
ugal at war with France in 1214, orders the Chief Magistrate
to fortify Ypres. "

On the opposite side of the hall, the spaces between the
window the mural decorations consisted of emblematic and

61 YPRES — THE HALLES — ROOM PAUWELS

heraldic paintings, together with copies of charters, etc., and
the whole formed a noble setting for the official banquets,
receptions and concerts which used to be given here.

On the other side of the Belfry, whose first floor was a
small square chamber between double lancet arches spring-
ing from the middle columns, stretched the Salle Delbeke.
Here the decorative artist did not enjoy the advantage of
great panels between the supporting timber, but the designs
were a happy blending of design and colour, symbolising the
phases of life and progress in the ancient town, such as Inde-
pendence, Commerce, Manufacture, Charity, Literature, etc.
Unhappily, the painter died before the completion of his
work.

Returning through the eastern apartment, the visitor
reached a doorway leading into the justly celebrated Salle
Echevinale or Aldermanic chamber, some fifty feet square
and 20 in height. It was lit by a large stained-glass window,
with the coats of arms of the old guilds, while opposite
stood a magnificent and monumental Flemish chimney piece,
carved by Malfait of Brussels. On the walls were several
wonderful old mural paintings, discovered, after long being
hidden under whitewash, in 1841. These designs and
portraits of great historic interest were executed from 1322
to 1468. Other later paintings and carved woodwork
further distinguished the room. The courtyard of the Town
Hall, although a small space hemmed in between the buildings to the north, was yet very interesting and picturesque.
The quaint overhanging offices, the elaborate wooden gables
of the Great Hall and the bulk of the noble belfry looming
above, combined to lend a charm to this vanished courtyard.

To the north of the Cloth Hall stand the magnificent ruins
of the Cathedral Church of St. Martin. This building was
erected in the thirtheenth century, on the
ST. MARTIN'S site of a former church built in 1073 by
CHURCH   Count Robert the Frisian. This church
endured until the wealth and importance of
Ypres made a greater edifice necessary.

The choir dates from 1221, belonging to the period of transition from the Romanesque to the pointed style. This portion of St. Martin's was pronounced by Schayes in his

YPRES — ST MARTIN CHURCH

History of Architecture as the grandest and most imposing example of ecclesiastical architecture in Belgium. The nave and transepts, begun in 1254 took twelve years to complete. They were in pure Gothic style, but before the war the

YPRES — INTERIOR OF ST MARTIN CHURCH

exterior stonework and flying buttresses were showing signs of delapidation. The south porch dates from the early fifteenth century and contained a large rose window of much beauty.

The Tower, although never fully completed, was 188 feet in height, of massive construction, built in 1433. It was entered on the north side and the ascent was made by a well-lighted winding staircase of 343 steps. From the summit a superb view of the surrounding country was obtained.

The first impression on entering the Church was the loftiness of the nave and the harmonious proportions of the whole structure. The lenght of the Church was 316 feet. Around the walls extended a beautiful triforium. The choir was without collateral chapels or ambulatory. The carved wooden stalls in Renaissance style dated from 1598. Above the high altar was a painting, " The Assumption ", by Luca Giordano. A series of tombs ran around the choir. One was that of Dame Louisa de Laye, widow of William Hugonnet, Viscount of Ypres, Chancellor of the Order of St. Mary of Burgundy, who was executed by the revolted burghers of Ghent, April 3rd. 1476 ; another was that of Martin Rythovius, first Bishop of Ypres, who ministered to the ill-fated Counts Egmont and Horn on the scaffold.

At the base of the altar reposed a small stone slab marked with a cross and the date 1638. Here is the resting place of the celebrated Cornelius Janssen (Jansenius), seventh Bishop of Ypres, whose posthumous work on *Grace* gave rise to the sect of Jansenists.

Close at hand was another marble slab denoting the burial place of Robert of Bethune, Count of Flanders, who died at Ypres in 1322. Formerly there was a splendid mausoleum here to his memory, but this perished at the hands of the Reformation mobs,

On the left of the choir was the chapel of our Lady of Thuyne, the Patroness of Ypres, with a gilded reredos. Here was also a fifteenth century painting of the siege of Ypres in 1318, showing the uniforms then worn by the four Guilds and armed fraternities of Ypres (St. Sebastian, St. George, St. Michael and St. Barbara).

Beneath the rose window hung an enormous painting, 'The Triumph of the Blessed Sacrament', by a native of Ypres, Nicholas Vandenvelde (1649-1732). The pulpit was most elaborate, as may be seen in the illustration page 15. Over it was inscribed the date 1255 and an inscription in old Flemish.

In the porch beneath the Tower was a fine triumphal arch around which were grouped the hatchments of the eighteen

YPRES — ST MARTIN CHURCH
MARBLE SCREEN WITH BRONZE BALUSTRADES

bishops of Ypres. The south aisle was separated from the little chapel of St. Anne and the chapel of the Dean by a fine Renaissance marble screen with bronze balustrades and alabaster figures. Within the Dean's chapel was, amongst other paintings, a large one representing 'the siege of Ypres by the Spanish in 1649' by F. P. Hals.

North of the Cathedral one passed through an Ionic gateway bearing the inscription 'Claustrum Sancti Martini', a fragment of which still stands. It marks the entrance to the old St. Martin's Cloisters. Here to the right were the interesting

remains of an ancient building (14th. century) part of the
former Abbey of St. Martin's founded in 1102 by Pope Pascal
II. The building came latterly to be used as a store-room
and theatre. South of it, nearer the Church, was the Place
Vandenpeereboom (Pear-tree) named in recent times after
the Belgian statesman (1884) whose statue was erected here.
This open space was a filled-in dock and formerly the inner
port of Ypres at a time when the Yperlee flowed openly
past the Church and town. There were within the past
century some old gabled houses still standing half hidden
behind modern ones. To the west of the Cloth Hall one in
particular attracted many tourists. Within the square of the
Cathedral stood the old Poor Clare's convent, a large and
not very beautiful structure. In front of it was the Bishop's
Palace (18th. century) latterly used as the Law Courts.
Adjoining it was the Bibliotheque or Public Library, full of
precious volumes and parchments. But the gem of all this
group of buildings was the Cloisters, of which exquisite traces
                                        still remain. To the East was the
THE CLOISTERS Petite Conciergerie which was rebuilt
                                        in 1633 in the style of the Nieuwerck.
Here from 1418 onwards the Aldermen and Town officials had
their banqueting chamber. During the French occupation
the Petite Conciergerie was sold for a tavern which retained
the old name. Close to it were two picturesque gabled
houses.

In the Rue de Dixmude (No. 54) still stands the façade of
a typical and most interesting Ypres mansion, the maison
Biebuyck, with the date in iron numerals thereupon, 1544.
Other notable houses in the same street were nos, 66 and
81 with Dorique façade of the 17th. century. In the
Nouveau Chemin St. Martin was the ancient Beguinage,
latterly used as a gendarmerie.

Nearly opposite the Cloth Hall stood the Boucherie or
Meat Market, a double gabled Gothic house with lower
stories of stone dating from the 13th. century. On the first

floor was the Municipal Museum, filled with paintings, carvings and curiosities, amongst them the archive chest of the Clothmakers (formerly kept in the Belfry).

YPRES — MEAT MARKET

Close at hand runs southward, the Rue de Lille, the widest and longest of the streets of Ypres. On

RUE DE LILLE the right stood the old chapel of the Hospice Belle, an asylum for old women

3

founded in 1279 by the pious widow of Solomon Belle and rebuilt in 1616. On either side of the façade was a niche (still visible) containing the kneeling statues of husband and

YPRES — FRONT OF THE HOSPICE BELLE

wife. In the ante-chapel were some fifteenth century grave-stones. Behind the chapel were the offices of the Board of

Almshouses of Ypres, one of the wealthiest in Belgium since it was in receipt of donations and legacies from the 12th. century. Just before the Great War its income amounted to over £20,000 sterling and it administered a number of local charities.

Continuing down the Rue de Lille you came upon the Hotel Merghelynck at the corner of **HOTEL MERGHELYNCK** the Marché-aux-Vieux Habits (Old Clothes Market), built in 1774 by François Merghelynck. Counsellor-Treasurer of Ypres — a typical 18th. century mansion in the French style. In 1891 this house was fitted up as a private museum, to illustrate the furniture, decoration and domestic life of the 18th. century, and was filled from kitchen to attic — 30 rooms in all — with mantel-pieces, beds, tables, spinets, chairs, china, books, drawings and engravings, exactly as if the whole house were in daily use, even to the 18th. century clothes hanging in the closets or thrown over a chair. The illusion was very striking.

Further down this street stand the ruins of a tall old building once called the Steenen, dating from the 14th. century. For centuries it had been known as the House of the Templars. For it was at Ypres that the Knights Templar had their first habitation in continental Europe. We know that in 1127 Geoffrey de St. Omers, one of the founders, built a dwelling near the Porte du Temple. **TEMPLARS HOUSE** Whatever the building's origin it was of the same style as the Cloth Hall, the same rectangular openings on the ground floor, the same pointed windows, the same battlement surmounting the wall and the same flanking turrets at the corners. It may well have had the same architect.

In 1897 the Belgian Government bought the building (which had been used as a brewery) and converted it into the Post Office restoring the front and making certain additions.

In the Rue de Lombard was a large building dated 1665,

formerly the Municipal Mont de Piété (Pawnshop) called
" The Lombard ". It was the Lombards who first in Europe
took up the trade of lending money on chattels, etc.

                          On the East side of the Rue de Lille are
ST. PETER'S the ruins of the Church of St. Peter, built in
    CHURH   1073 by Robert the Frisian. In the course
                          of more than eight centuries this Church
underwent many changes, but the ancient Romanesque tower
remained until the bombardment, and the principal porch, of

YPRES — PANORAMA

great archeological interest, still stands. This was the
Church of the brave Curé Delaere (now Dean of Ypres)
whose labours during the bombardment won him the love and
admiration of the people and of our troops.

Opposite St. Peter's formerly stood a quaint pair of medieval houses. When one of them was demolished to widen
the street, a local chronicler wrote (1913) despairingly :
" Thus little by little every trace of local character is disap-
pearing. One might ask why it is that local builders do not
use the local models. The old Ypres style of building has
a charm of its own and lends itself to the requirements of
modern hygiene and comfort ". Poor Ypres ! The Great
War swept it all away and to judge by the crude and bizarre
erections since, the Ypres tradition is little valued by the
present race of Yprians.

A little farther down the Rue de Lille on the right at the
end of a narrow lane might have been seen a yellow gable
capped by an elegant hexagonal bell-turret. This was the
Hospice Ste. Godelieve, founded in 1277 for the reception of
pilgrims who used to flock into Ypres through the Lille
gate. Since 1812 it served as an almshouse for 48 aged
infirm women. Within were some antique
furniture and several paintings by Karl
van Yper. The Nun's workroom was a
large rectangular panelled chamber fur-
nished in Renaissance style and with a fine painting over the
ornate mantelpiece.

YPRES
LACE-MAKING

Hereabouts was the centre of the Ypres lace-making —
and hundreds of women and girls might have been seen at
the doors of their houses, the cushion and bobbins in their
laps, gossiping or singing ancient tunes.

At the end of the street stood a famous picturesque wooden
house, a solitary relic of the days when most of the Flemish
houses were built entirely of wood. Many attempts were
made to remove it, but the archaeologist gained the day and
it remained for the German shells to effect the destruction.

And now we come to the Lille Gate. This was fortified
by three massive semicircular towers, erected in 1395. A
wide stone bridge crossed the deep moat. The ramparts,
chiefly built by Vauban, with their thick
stone walls continue from here around the
eastern front of the town. To gain a good
view of the old fortifications which, although they bore the
brunt for four years of much German heavy metal, were never
really pierced, the visitor should cross the bridge and
turning to the left follow the circular road as far as the
Menin Gate. Or he can proceed by a pathway just within
the Lille Gate to the summit of the ramparts, where a path
will conduct him to the same point. If the path is taken
most of the Ypres Salient is visible, and note should

LILLE GATE

particularly be made of the pond of ZILLEBEKE a couple
of miles to the south east of the town, which was dug in 1295
and down to within living memory furnished the principal
source of water supply to Ypres.   Zillebeke and its sur-
roundings are a famous battlefield.   Halfway behind the
ramparts between the Lille and Menin Gates stood St. James's
Church, beside which, in the old army bakery, so many British
divisions and brigades had their head-quarters (St. Jacques)
during the Great War.   The Church dates from 1139, but
the tower and other parts were not completed before 1412.

Crossing westward by the ruins of the Church and the
adjacent convents (amongst them the Carmelites, St. Joseph's
and the Irish Nuns) we reach the Rue de St. Jacques, which
had some very interesting houses.   One
ST. JACQUES (No. 14) built in 1769 boasted a fine bal-
cony.   The next street parallel westward
is the Rue des Chiens where still may be seen the double-
gabled remains of the finest houses in Ypres — formerly
the Hotel de Gand, but a private residence at the outbreak of war.

The Grand'Place, to which we are now returned, had long
been a scene of peace and comparative solitude.   Since its
medieval glories and sufferings — since the martial bustle of
later wars — Ypres was an almost preternaturally quiet
town and its great market-place reflected its spirit. Save on
Saturdays ; and then the wide expanse became filled with
vans, carts and stalls.   The Ypres butter-market was the
largest in Flanders, the peasants came from leagues round
about and as many as 20,000 kilos of butter changed hands
during the morning — most of it going across the borders
to France.

The large building on the East side of the Grand'Place
was the Hôpital Notre Dame.   The site was given to the
town in 1187 by Phillip of Alsace, Count of Flanders to erect
a building for the sick poor of Ypres.   Within were several
interesting tombs and paintings.

YPRES — CATTLE MARKET — GUILDHOUSES

On the northern side of the square was the Hotel de la
Chatellenie which was once the headquarters of the civil admi-
nistrative district of Ypres, prior to the French Revolution.

Further on, down the Rue Surmont de Volsberghe, we
reach the old Cattle Market (Marché au Bétail) which, like
the Place Vandenpeereboom, was an old filled-in quay. Here
were three old Guildhouses, one of the Watermen which bore
two carved medallions showing ships in full sail. To the
west in the Rue d'Elverdinghe was a fine old Gothic house
(No. 33) formerly a convent. The large building on the
north is the Prison, the Town Major's office in war-time
and beyond is the great Water Tower dislodged by a shell.

Up to 1886 the walls and moat of the old fortifications
extended from the Prison to the Railway Station, but the
walls were then demolished and the moat filled in. Just east
of where the walls recommence is the Esplanade, or infantry
parade-ground. At the extremity of the latter stand the
ruins of the Infantry Barracks, built under the Dutch admin-
istration of Ypres. The garrison consisted of one Infantry

CAVALRY
BARRACKS

batallion and a Military College. Farther on
was the Cavalry barracks and Military School,
the chief one of the Belgian army and ranking
amongst the best in Europe. Every cavalry
officer in the Kingdom acquired his training in Ypres.

In one corner of the Esplanade was the headquarters of
the ancient Archery Guild of St. Sebastian, founded in 1302,
after the Battle of the Golden Spurs.

In the Rue au Beurre, which leads us again into the
Grand'Place is the ruin of the great Church of St. Nicholas,

ST. NICHOLAS

and close at hand stood the Fish
Market, with a carved entrance way.
Behind the Church was a turret forming
part of an Abbey founded at Ypres by the monks of
Therouane after the capture and destruction of their town in
1553. Seven or eight years before the war the two upper
stories of this tower were needlessly removed, and thus

exclains the local scribe, " Another witness of a glorious past disappears ! "

There were many other interesting buildings and shrines in Ypres of which the war has destroyed all trace. Of the new buildings close to the Grand'Place was the Bank of Courtrai whose spacious vaults provided bomb proof shelter for many distinguished officers during the bombardment. They can still be seen and entered to-day, revealing dozens of safety deposit coffers from which the valuables were only finally removed in the Spring ot 1915.

———

THE FIRST BATTLE OF

YPRES

At 11 o'clock, on the morning of Wednesday, the 7th.
October 1914, YPRES for the first time heard those guns of
war which were to encompass her destruction. Two hours
later the first shell descended on the town.

Some German cavalry and cyclists suddenly appeared in
the Grand'Place. They were the vanguard of a retreating
host whom the victory of the Allies on the Marne had inter-
rupted in their march to Calais and the English Channel.

But on that day also Antwerp, the great Belgian
fortress which was firmly believed to be impregnable, was
doomed. A mighty German army was sweeping all before
it, and before night fell the population was fleeing madly for
safety to the roar of the monster guns. In a few hours the
fleeing German force in Flanders would effect a junction
with the victors of Antwerp, and all Belgium and
Northern France would, it seemed, be in their hands. To
meet the invaders and push back the German force which
was retreating, Field Marshal Sir John French, Commander-
in-Chief of the British Army, was hurrying forward two army
corps, so as to reach Bruges, Menin, Lille and La
Bassée, isolate General von Beseler's army and cut it off
between Lille and the sea. This was the main point of
that early October strategy for us and the foe, to reach the
battle ground first.

In addition to the two British corps, the nucleus of
another corps, consisting of the 7th. division and the 3rd.
Cavalry division, landed at Ostend and Zeebrugge on

October 8th. and began rapidly moving southward to join
up with our troops moving north. Thus was witnessed the
retreat of the Belgian army westward from Antwerp and
the retirement of the foiled German force eastward from
CASSEL, HAZEBROUK and BAILLEUL. When Antwerp fell on October 9th. the British Cavalry under
General Byng had left Zeebrugge and was sweeping
down to THOUROUT and ROULERS, while Sir Douglas
Haig and the First Corps were coming up from the south-
west pushing the enemy before them.

In Ypres on that day 20,000 Germans entered the town.
With them were 600 cannon, 1300 machine-guns and enormous quantities of munitions. The German General summoned
M. Colaert, the burgomaster and informed him that his army
would occupy the town for three days and that during that
time the inhabitants must be quiet and keep within doors.
Any act of hostility would be certain death. To guarantee
good behaviour the burgomaster, the aldermen and certain
notable citizens were held hostage. Moreover, the sum of
70,000 francs was instantly exacted, which happened to be
five thousand more than there was in the municipal treasury.
During their brief sojourn in Ypres the Germans left many
marks of their character, amongst other exploits pillaging
several jewellery, clothing and grocery shops. Within the
walls of one Belgian institution they quartered 30 horses and
left upon the wall this legend : " The Germans fear God, and
nothing else in the world. Deutschland uber alles ! "

They departed in haste and confusion through the Lille
Gate, for General Pulteney and the 3rd. Corps and General
Allenby's cavalry corps were close at their heels. On Tuesday, the 13th. October, the first British advance guard
entered Ypres and were received joyously by the inhabitants
and thereafter for several days the troops began moving
through.

Little did they or their commander know what was await-
ing them. They were full of spirits and fancied that victory

was close at hand. Not yet did they realise the extent of the
disaster of Antwerp. Nor did they know that a mighty
German host, many times the size of that they had routed,
was coming to meet them. Not even Sir John French realised
the position, but he ordered General Haig to push on through
Ypres. "The object he is to have in view," he wrote,
"is the capture of Bruges and subsequently if possible to
drive the enemy towards Ghent". "I am free to con-

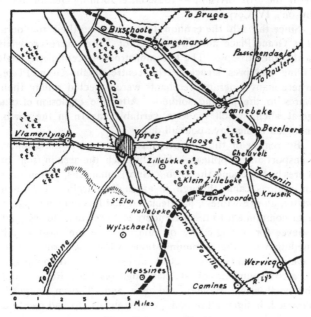

FIRST BATTLE OF YPRES

fess," wrote Sir John French afterwards, "that on October
15th. 1914, the day upon which I date the opening of the
Battle of Ypres, I thought the danger was passed. I believed that the enemy had exhausted his strength in the great

bid he had made to smash our arms on the Marne and to capture Paris. "

So the First Corps of the " contemptible little British army " (as the Kaiser termed it) passed light-heartedly through the Menin Gate. It was not alone. It had on its left Bidon's divisions of French Territorials and Cavalry, reaching from BIXSCHOOTE north through HOUTHULST Forest. On its right was Byng's Cavalry division joining up with the 7th. division — these latter forming General Rawlinson's IV. Corps.

Since the 9th. the cannon had not ceased their thunders. The Grand'Place and the streets of Ypres were crowded with Allied troops. The first monstrous 42 centimetre shell falling on Ypres struck in the centre of the Grand'Place, where many itinerant merchants were collected selling their wares to the passing soldiers. After the explosion of this great shell, which made a veritable cavern in the earth, mangled bodies lay about all day.

By reason of the topographical figuration of the country, transport and supplies could only reach the area in front of Ypres by traversing the town. Guns, munitions, ambulances and rations came through in an endless train. A French writer, an eye-witness, has declared that he could not pay a finer compliment to the defenders of Ypres than to say that " never for a single day or hour despite the most terrific shelling were the communications, whose stoppage would have ensured a German victory, arrested. " And now began to arrive numbers of Belgian fugitives from Roulers and the north-east. Women, old men and children, fatigued, harassed, hungry, all hoped, poor wretches, to find rest and peace in Ypres.

Peace and rest ! Not again, for nearly a lustrum, would there be peace and rest in Ypres. Ascend that first week of October 1914, to the summit of the church tower and look out over the plain where these hosts were assembling. Descry the autumn landscape, the pleasant villages dotted

here and there.   ST. JEAN, WIELTJE, LANGEMARCK,
ST. JULIEN, POELCAPELLE, HOOGHE, ZONNEBEKE,
GHELUVELT, the picturesque old chateaux, the thick
forests and graceful parks, the shining lakes and ornamental
waters, as they were this October day.   You are looking
upon them for the last time.   Never again will they be as
they were.   The whole of this happy undulating segment of
land is doomed.   For it is to be the most stupendous battle-
ground in all history.   It is to be drenched in blood.   Every
town, every village is to be uprooted ; every dwelling is to be
demolished ; every tree of every grove is to be destroyed for
ever.   Nothing in the whole of this extensive plain is to be
spared and desolation unspeakable is, like a pall, to over-
spread the land.   One thing only is to survive, and that, as
long as England and Englishmen live, can never die — the
memory of the deaths of millions of brave soldiers fighting in
the cause of all humanity, an eternal flame of glory which
shines about this sepulchre of our heroic dead.

On October 19th. the British advance ceased in this sector
of the line and the YPRES SALIENT was born.   It was
now clear to the Higher Command that the main German
front had been reached — a front extending from Lille to
the sea.   The First Division had got as far as a line drawn
from Bixschoote to Langemarck, the Second Division
continuing the line to the cross-roads a mile and a
half north west of Zonnebeke.   Here it touched Byng's
3rd. Cavalry Division, upon whose right lay the 7th. Division,
through Becelaere to a point on the Menin Road east of
the Gheluvelt cross-roads.   South of Zandvoorde was
Allenby and his Cavalry corps, fresh from the capture of
MESSINES.   The III. Corps continued ten miles further
south through ARMENTIÈRES.   Both sides were in readiness — a battle was imminent.   The main thrust came on
Oct. 21st. against the apex of the salient between Zonnebeke and BECELAERE.   Haig's First Corps were stead-

ily advancing at 2 p.m. when news came that the French
Territorials had been driven by the Germans out of the forest
of Houthulst and were with the supporting French Cavalry
retreating across the Ypres canal. The 7th. Division
and Allenby's Cavalry, heavily attacked, were forced to
halt. Lawford's 22nd. Brigade of this Division was enfiladed and for a time its flank was in danger, until the 2nd.
Division linked up with it at the Ypres-Roulers railway
crossing.

The 21st. Brigade (Watts) was holding Becelaere which
was, as has been said, the point of the newly formed
salient. Here the Germans thrust powerfully in between the
Royal Scots Fusiliers and the Yorkshires ; but the cold steel
checked them. At the same time a staff officer dashed down
the Menin Road to Haig at Hooghe Chateau to say that
the enemy was threatening to break through the line southward at KLEINE ZILLEBEKE held by Gough's 2nd. Cavalry Division. Kavanagh's 7th. Cavalry Brigade, the only
reserves available, were ordered to fling themselves into the
breach, which they did and held on until the 2nd. Division
could come up. Towards nightfall Byng's whole Cavalry
Division was shifted from near St. Julien to about HOLLE-
BEKE on the right of the 7th. Division, joining up with
Gough's troops.

The situation was now critical. A divided command was
seen to be a source of great danger. The French Territorials who had retired at Bixschoote were not under
the British Commander-in-chief. Thousands of them had
swarmed into Ypres filling the town. Lord French says,
" I was so strongly impressed with the danger of the confusion and congestion which the divided command was causing in the north that I went myself on the evening of the
21st. to Ypres, where I was met by Haig, Rawlinson, de
Mitry and Bidon, and arrangements were then made by
which the town was to be at once cleared of the French
troops and the left flank of the 1st. Corps properly covered."

Joffre the French Commander-in-chief also visited Sir
John, who told him he was immediately bringing up the 9th.
French Army Corps to Ypres to act under his orders.
Also that same night two battalions of Indian troops (Lahore
Division) were sent forward in motor omnibuses to WUL-
VERGHEM to act with Allenby's Cavalry.

Heavy fighting was resumed next day. Repeated and
bloody enemy assaults were made to break through the line.
North of PILKEM the Camerons held the trenches which
had been indifferently dug by the French Territorials.   Part
of this famous regiment — the 'red tartans' of Quatre Bras
and Tel-el-Kebir — proceeded to turn a wayside tavern into
a fortress.   When the enemy broke through they found
themselves cut off, and for a time it looked as if they would
be exterminated to a man.

Moreover, the gap between the Royal Scots Fusiliers and
the Yorkshires (21st. Brigade) already spoken of, still existed
and indeed continued for three days — the Yorkshires having to do fierce battle on a double front.   The fighting raged
about Hollebeke where, with his superior infantry and
artillery and large numbers of snipers, it seemed as if our
cavalry fighting on foot must be pressed back.   But they had
splendid leadership in Byng and Gough, and they held firm.

Trench warfare on a big scale had begun.   But the
trenches were not the trenches we came to know.   The
British soldier had yet to realise the value of deep spade
work.   He disliked — and to the end disliked — the duty of
digging.   It was not his notion of fighting.   As a poet then
wrote:

> It is not meet that Englishmen
> Should lurk and stoop and crawl;
> Better be what we have been
> Than cringe behind a wall.
> Better in one wild charge to die
> If death can quicken victory!

4

The early trenches, then, were little better than ditches ; and soon these ditches became filled with water, and the embankments, slimy and treacherous heaps of mud, fell in.

There was to be no rest or respite for the First Corps, who had already borne the brunt of the fighting on the Aisne. The 23rd. of October dawned, the 22nd. Brigade had failed to hold on, which caused a sharp point in the line at Becelaere on the left of the 7th. Division. During the day Major General Bulfin, leading the Royal West Surreys, the Northamptons and the King's Royal Rifles, drove back the Germans and rescued the imprisoned Cameronians at the point of the bayonet. 600 Germans were captured. Near Langemarck to the left, held by the 3rd. Brigade, the enemy massed his troops, who came on with extraordinary courage and *élan*. Our artillery received them furiously ; they recoiled, but in spite of thinning ranks avanced again and again. That night 1500 German dead lay about Langemarck and the enemy's efforts had ended in failure.

Our troops were worn out at last, and were glad when two divisions of troops from the IX. French Corps (just returned from Rheims) appeared upon the scene and took over the trenches of our 2nd. Division. The latter could not yet rest, for they were sent to the relief of the much tried 7th. Division who were being pressed about Zonnebeke. Troops of that Division, the Bedfords, had succeeded in closing the breach between the Yorkshires and the Scots Fusiliers and so a little relieving the strain which had fallen on the Wiltshires, who held the very apex of the Salient, and also on the adjoining Warwicks.

On the following day (24th.) the troops were cheered by the tidings that the French IX. Corps veterans had succeeded in winning ground between Zonnebeke and Poelcapelle and that the French Territorials had rallied and relieved our weary 1st. Division who were marched down behind Zillebeke. On this day the Second Division moved up

First Prisonners in Ypres

so as to form contact with the 7th. Division : and none too soon ! For the Wiltshires fighting like heroes at the apex of the Salient had been pushed back with heavy losses and the enemy reached a corner of the Polygon Wood just west of Becelaere. In vain the Warwicks (22nd. Brigade) counter-attacked, losing their Colonel (Loring) and many officers. The Germans could not be dislodged. But at least the expected did not happen ; they did not advance, and our counter-offensive on the left continued to relieve the pressure on the point of the Salient. That night the enemy massed his troops before KRUSEIK, n. e. of Zand-voorde — in the South of the Salient — and broke through. But the feat cost him dear — the incoming horde was cut off and 200 prisoners were made. Undaunted, however, by this, the enemy renewed his assault at dawn, and this time the brunt was borne by the Scots Guards, who suffered heavily. For a time it seemed as if the foe had found the vulnerable point he sought at last and must gain the Zandvoorde ridge. It was a fateful moment. In the early afternoon (27th.) the 7th. Cavalry Brigade were led to a counter-attack. In the van were the Blues, under Colonel Gordon Wilson, who pushed back the Germans towards the hamlet of AMERICA on the Wervicq road and so saved the situation.

While this was happening a readjustment of the British line was decided upon at the head-quarters at Hooghe. In the Chateau, lately the charming country-seat of the Baron de Vinck, Sir John French, Sir Douglas Haig and Sir Henry Rawlinson held an anxious consultation. The weakness lay in the 7th. Division which was tired out with incessant fighting and depleted by slaughter. It held a most critical place in the line, that between Gheluvelt and east of Zand-voorde. It was accordingly resolved to break up the IV. Corps, send General Rawlinson to England to supervise the preparations of the 8th. Division and attach the 7th. Division to Haig (I. Corps). Byng's 3rd. Cavalry Division would be merged into Allenby's force.   So the gallant 7th. were put in south of the Menin Road, not for rest, but to await developments.

For on the 28th. it was manifest by many signs that the enemy was preparing to launch a thunderbolt. There was little or no infantry fighting that day in the Salient although the guns were never silent. The next day, the 29th., the storm of battle broke in its fury. " At 9 in the morning, " says Lord French, " the centre of the Ypres Salient, held by the 1st. and 7th. Divisions, was attacked in the neigh-bourhood of Gheluvelt by large masses of the enemy who forced back our troops on the latter place. Throughout the morning the wave of battle ebbed and flowed. From La Bassée to the sea 12 German corps were opposed to seven of the Allies ". In addition was the enemy enormously superior in artillery. But the brunt of the fighting this day fell on our I. corps which had to meet the German XIII. and XV. Corps and the 2nd. Bavarian Division. But the onslaught extended all along the line south to LE GHIER beyond Messines. After a day of carnage the 1st. and 7th. Divisions had regained all the ground they had earlier lost. The line of the Salient was now well to the east of Gheluvelt, and so represented a clear gain. REUTEL and POEZEL-HOEK were held by the enemy (XXVII. Reserve corps and 6th. Bavarian Division) who faced our 2nd. Division, who in turn east of Zonnebeke station, joined up with the IX. French corps.

With dawn on the 30th. the fierce battle was resumed.

An hour later Haig reported that he was being heavily shelled all along his front and that the enemy was moving in great force to attack Byng's 3rd. Cavalry Division on his right. Gough had sent two regiments and a battery of horse artillery to support Byng. One of these regiments (the Royal Dragoons) had with great dash and gallantry repulsed an attack on the Chateau at Hollebeke.

But the weight of enemy metal was against us. Whole

trenches disappeared. One troop was buried alive. Byng's
Cavalry had to fall back, and the right of the 2nd. Division
being left uncovered, the troops had likewise to retire. This
still further sharpened the point of the Salient at Gheluvelt.

" Hearing heavy firing towards Ypres I went to Haig's
headquarters at Hooghe " states Lord French. " Whilst I
was with Haig, Allenby came in. It appeared that strong
forces were attacking the 3rd. and 2nd. Cavalry Divisions
around Hollebeke.   Allenby had sent a brigade to support
Gough who had also been obliged to recall the support
he had proviously sent to Byng. Haig had sent the
London Scottish to support Gough and had brought down
Bulfin with most of the 2nd. Brigade to strengthen the 7th.
Division on his right. "

But this was not enough.   The situation grew very critical.
Sir Douglas Haig determined that the line from Gheluvelt
to the angle of Ypres-Comines Canal south of Klein Zillebeke must be kept at all hazards.   For if the enemy reached
the canal at any point north of Hollebeke the communications of the I. corps would forthwith be severed and Ypres
would lie at their mercy.

At this juncture the Emperor William II makes a dramatic
appearance.   He is in the midst of his troops at Menin
making a speech to the Bavarians. The capture of Ypres
— so runs the Imperial announcement — will settle the issue
of the war.   Take Ypres, and Calais and the Channel ports
will be in the hands of the Fatherland !

The chief peril lay then at Klein Zillebeke. But
on the right the 2nd. Cavalry Division had already been
forced from Hollebeke to ST. ELOI, and Messines, held
by the 1st. Cavalry Division was being heavily shelled
by enemy howitzers. On Haig's left the 6th. Brigade (1st.
Battalion, King's Liverpool Regiment, 2nd. battalions South
Staffs, the 1st. Berks and first Kings Royal Rifles) was thrice
attacked during the day. Once the German infantry reached
the new barbed wire entanglements in front of the trenches.

On the left of the 1st. Corps on the Yser heavy fighting continued all day. Night fell and still the issue remained undecided.

But a decision was not far off. At 2 a.m., on the fateful 31st. October General Foch visited Sir John French and promised to let him have as support for Haig five French battalions of artillery. At dawn the battle was renewed on the Menin road against Gheluvelt. The first Brigade (containing the Coldstreams) and the 3rd. Brigade were flung back fighting so desperately that when the famous Guards took toll of the losses it was found that only a handful of unwounded survivers answered the call. Back the whole Division was slowly forced to the woods between VELD-HOEK and Hooghe. At the same time the British Cavalry were driven out of Messines and terrific fighting went on there all day.

The retirement of the 1st. Division (Lomax) threatened the flank of the 7th. Division. Owing to this the Royal Scots Fusiliers (50 Brigade) who refused to leave their trenches without orders were enveloped and cut off. A few weeks before this Battalion had landed in Flanders over a thousand strong ; after this terrible ordeal they mustered but 70 men and their only officer was a junior subaltern.

General Lomax, threatened with a general rout, had ordered his reserves to hold the east edge of the woods and was concerting further measures when at 1.15 p.m. his Division headquarters and that of the 2nd. Division at Hooghe were shelled. The general was struck and some staff officers were killed. General Monro (2nd. Division) was ordered to take command of the 1st. Division. And now what happened is best told in Lord French's own words.

" As I passed through Ypres on my way to Haig, there were manifest signs of unusual excitement, and some shells were already falling in the place. It is wonderful with what rapidity the contagion of panic spreads through a civilian population. I saw loaded vehicles leaving the town, and people gathered in groups about the streets chattering like monkeys, or rushing hither and thither with frightened faces.

" As we passed by the ancient Cloth Hall, the old Cath-edral, and other splendid examples of Flemish architecture for which this town was famed, I did not realise how soon the atmosphere of German " frightfulness " was to reduce all those noble buildings to a heap of ruins.

" On reaching the eastern exit of the town, on my way Hooghe, I was stopped by a guard specially posted by First Corps Headquarters, with orders te prevent anyone leaving the city.

" Satisfying them as to my indentity, I proceeded on my way. I had not gone more than a mile when the traffic on the road began to assume a most anxious and threatening appea-rance. It looked as if the whole of the I. Corps was about to fall back in confusion on Ypres. Heavy howitzers were moving west at a trot, always a most significant feature of a retreat, and ammunition and other wagons blocked the road almost as far as the eye could reach. In the midst of the press of traffic, and both sides of the road, crowds of wounded men came limping along as fast as they could go, all heading for Ypres. Shells were screaming overhead and bursting with reverberating explosions in the adjacent fields.

" This filled me with misgiving and alarm. It was imposs-ible for my motor-car to proceed at any pace, so we alighted and covered the rest of the way to Haig's Headquarters on foot, nor did I receive any encouragement on the way to hope for better things.

" The chateau of Hooghe, where 1st. Army Headquarters were situated, has long since been erased from the face of the earth in the severe fighting which has raged about it. But as I found it on that October afternoon, it was a typical modern red brick chateau, approached by a gate and a short avenue from the road.   Shells were falling about the place, and the chateau was already beginning to show the effects of artillery fire.

" I found Haig and John Gough, his Chief of Staff, in one

of the rooms on the ground floor, poring over maps and
evidently much disconcerted. But, though much perturbed
in mind and very tired in body and brain, Haig was cool and
alert as ever. Both he and Gough gave me a bad account of
the state of affairs. "

" ... The worst news was that the 1st. Division had broken
back and were in full retreat, only a mile or so to the east of
where we were standing, with the Germans at their heels...
I felt as if the last barrier between the Germans and the
Channel seaboard was broken down and I viewed the
situation with the utmost gravity.

It was a dramatic half hour, the worst I ever spent.

It had a truly dramatic climax. At about 3 p.m, a staff
officer galloped up to the front of the chateau with the news
that the 1st. Division had rallied and again moved forward.
Gheluvelt was once more in our hands ! "

At 3.30 p.m. Gheluvelt had been retaken at the point
of the bayonet by the 2nd. Worcesters who were in
reserve to the 2nd. Division. Grasping like a flash the
gravity of the situation Brigadier General Charles Fitz
Clarence V. C. commanding the 1st. Guards Brigade seeing
how badly the battle was going on on the right of the Scots
Guards, borrowed the 2nd Worcesters from the 2nd Division
on his own responsibility to counterattack.

" By shoving us in at the time and place he did " afterwards declared the battalion commander, " the General
saved the day. If he had waited, I don't think I could have
got the battalion up in time to save the South Wales Borderers and fill the gap. "

A week later this brilliant officer Fitz Clarence was killed
in another part of the Salient.

This dramatic restoration of the British line set free the
6th. Cavalry Brigade who after clearing out the chateau
woods east of Gheluvelt filled the breach between the 7th.
Division and the 2nd. Brigade. Before night the dents in
the Salient had been made good.

Next day when new French reinforcements (XVI. Corps and I. Cavalry Corps) came up in relief, the enemy displayed his anger by heavy shelling.

" In Ypres from October 30th. " writes the devoted nun, (Sister Marguerite of Ypres) " we had judged it prudent to lodge on the ground floor of our house. Now we passed the nights in the cellar. Those who had no cellar took refuge in the casements of the ramparts. Those who were killed near us we buried in the Convent garden, for the shells did not permit us to gain the civil cemetery, and over the graves of the soldiers we raised a poor wooden cross, marked with the names of those beneath. "

The brave sister mentions that the first British soldier they buried in Ypres (Oct. 22nd.) was Private Whitehead of the Royal Warwicks.

In the bombardment of Nov. 1st. Messines was virtually destroyed and our troops were beaten back and WYTSCHAETE was also lost for a few hours until our Cavalry and the French retook it. There were many brave deeds performed, for which several awards of the Victoria Cross were made. Not least amongst them was that of young Dent of the East Lancashires who, when all his officers had fallen, took command of the platoon and held the position. But this was no uncommon occurrence. Extraordinary things happened. A Major commanded a platoon ; a Brigadier commanded one or two companies ; a subaltern found himself leading a battalion to assault. After the deprivation and tension of being pursued day and night by an infinitely stronger force the division (7th.) had now to pass through the worst ordeal of all.

On November 6th. at Klein Zillebeke the French under General Moussy on the right of our 2nd. and 4th. Brigades, were driven back and Lord Cavan's 4th. Brigade was left unsupported on its right flank. Byng's cavalry was hurriedly sent for, and with the aid of the 1st. and 2nd. Life

Guards, the French again came forward, the famous Blues
under Lt. Colonel Gordon Wilson in the rear. Still the
enemy came on and the French once more broke. Two
squadrons of the Blues flung themselves across the village
street which instantly became a scene of confusion and hand-
to-hand fighting. From the cottages poured forth a hot
rifle and machine gun fire and amongst those who fell was
the gallant Colonel of the Blues and Major Hon. Hugh
Dawnay, a brilliant officer, at the head of their men.

But the charge of the Household Cavalry at Klein
Zillebeke succeeded, and at least for a night the position
was held. But on the morrow, in spite of every effort the
line had to yield here a little to superior force. Elsewhere
our forces held firm, although of one brigade (Lawford's 22nd.)
only the commanding officer, five officers and 700 men
remained.

Then came a lull in the battle, but those four or five
days when our troops could at least breathe a little more
freely in the trenches saw no respite for Ypres. Nov. 7th. in
the afternoon witnessed an inferno of shelling. " Churches,
convents and public buildings were levelled to the ground.
Ten separate conflagrations broke out. "The city, " says
Sister Marguerite in her *journal*, " resembled an enormous furnace. " The little river Yperlee which ran under-
ground through the town was exposed at last to the light of
day. For several days Ypres was without bread or meat,
and the cellars were packed with poor folk half crazed with
terror, and with unburied dead. Moving amongst them
undaunted went the brave Curé Delaere and his little band
of nuns succouring the living and burying the dead. *

* A young Belgian Red Cross Worker (Mlle. Butaye) who returned to
Ypres, writes : " Pendant deux jours l'incendie a fait rage. Je n'aimerais
pas vous dire tout ce qu'on raconte parceque j'espère qu'il y a une immense
part d'exagération et je préfère vous dire plus tard ce que mes yeux
auraient vu ; mais en tout cas l'église St. Martin est en ruines ainsi que le
cloitre qui est effondré ; des Halles il reste une partie du beffroi jusqu'au
cadran, les Halles aux Viandes, musée et tout ce paté de maisons sont en

The few days cessation of fighting in the Salient was employed by the Germans in preparing their great and final effort of the First Battle of Ypres. So far the attempt to gain the city had failed. But surely nothing, reasoned the Kaiser, could withstand the Prussian Guards. And so, in imitation of Napoleon at Waterloo, the German War Lord brought up two brigades and 13 battalions from Arras as a supreme and definite measure to break through the allied line.

Down the road from Menin these marvellously disciplined battalions came — marching as if on parade — confident of snatching the victory their Emperor told them was theirs. Peering out at them from the Gheluvelt height, our men wondered but were not dismayed. There were the Kaiser Franz Grenadiers, the Queen Augusta Grenadiers, and the 1st, and 3rd. Footguards amongst this host. They were met by an accurate and appalling fire from our 1st. Division, but although they had to trample on their dead they advanced. Our troops fell back from Gheluvelt, the enemy took the woods to the west of our front line, including part of Polygon wood. But further they could not go. Our troops on both their flanks enfiladed them. Their losses were terrific, and at last they stopped and settled down in the trenches they had gained.

While thus the Salient was being pierced at its apex, to the left, General Dubois (IX. French corps) was fighting a life and death battle from Zonnebeke to Bixschoote, whose fields became heaped with corpses. Three German

cendre, le Vijfhoek en partie reste debout. Un paysan qui venait de traverser Ypres racontait qu'il s'était trouvé au milieu de la Place sans le savoir. Il n'y a plus moyen de s'y reconnaître tant il y a des ruines ; des quartiers entiers ont disparu.

Il y a encore bien du monde à Ypres mais dans les caves ; quelques vieux garçons et quelques héros se promènent dans les rues sous les obus; on cite le juge Gravez-Weckesser (le vieux) parmi les héros, Stoffel (un Dieu pour tous.) A. Ligy le commissaire de police, les curés de St-Pierre et de St-Jacques... "

regiments were annihilated one day and a fourth the next. The Wurtemburgers advanced in vain to envelop the town from north and south, but all his efforts ended in failure and by Nov. 15th. the Kaiser recognised that his high hopes had ended in disaster.

Here and there on the boundaries of the Salient desparate attacks were made twice in the south, but the line held, and by the 17th. November the weary British troops returning in a snow-storm from being relieved by French reinforcements, could tell the sentries at the ramparts that the great first Battle of Ypres was ended.

The three weeks battle had cost the Germans over 250,000 men. The Allies has lost over 100,000 including some of their best and most gallant officers.

"Scarcely a house famous in our stormy history but mourned a son. Wyndham, Dawnay, Fitz Clarence, Wellesley, Cadogan, Bruce, Gordon, Lennox, Fraser, Kinnaird, Hay, Hamilton ; it is like scanning the death-roll after Agincourt or Flodden." *

To the British Army had fallen the brunt of the fighting, and still the gateway to Calais was barred.

"The fact" says the German Staff Account, "that neither the enemy's commanders nor their troops gave way under the strong pressure we put on them, but continued to fight the battle round Ypres, though their situation was most perilous, gives us an opportunity to acknowledge that there were men of real worth opposed to us who did their duty thoroughly." **

---

* Buchan.

** YPRES, 1914. p. 71, British official translation, 1919.

THE SECOND BATTLE OF

YPRES

After the FIRST BATTLE OF YPRES, the British Army in the Salient were largely relieved by the French, who as the winter wore an — and it was a winter of almost unexempled severity — causing great suffering and mortality amongst the troops — were in turn relieved by the British. The 28th. Division in front of the town saw some very hard fighting in February. The Princess Patricia's, the first Canadian regiment to reach the front, had its baptism of fire at St. Eloi (February 28.) and greatly distinguished itself.

On April 17th. a bloody local conflict began which became world famous — the battle of Hill 60. The slight eminence so named is difficult for the visitor to distinguish to-day. It was an embankment some 50 feet high to 250 long near Klein Zillebeke on the north side of the Ypres-Comines railway. After taking over the sector from the French, General Smith-Darrien recognised the importance of capturing this hill, which was being used as a post of observation by the Germans. The engineers therefore set to work to mine it. Six tunnels were dug, each tunnel ending in a chamber containing a ton of explosive. At 7 p.m. on the 17th. the mines were fired, and while the deafening thunder was still reverberating and amidst the smoke, our infantry of the 23th. Brigade, darted forward from their trenches and occupied the hill. What Germans were there, shell-shocked and gasping, surrendered ; while 150 were buried in the debris. There was room for only one company on the summit, but sappers began at once digging trenches in the

rear. Soon after midnight the best part of two battalions
had dug themselves in in spite of showers of enemy bombs
which caused terrible casualties amongst the West Kents.
Early next morning the Scots Borderers went to relieve them,
followed, as the Germans showed signs of a strong counter-
attack, by other regiments. Soon after dawn the Germans
were close, with bombs and bayonets and there ensued a
scene of awful slaughter. Neither side would yield an inch
without a desperate effort. By 7 a.m. the enemy had gained

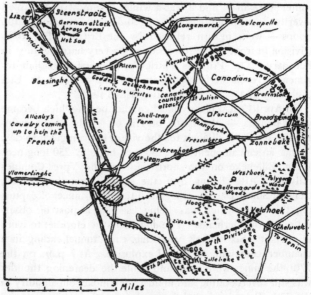

SECOND BATTLE OF YPRES

a foothold on part of the crest, while a few yards behind
them a gallant band of Yorkshiremen hung on grimly to the
craters and crevices in the side of the hill. At six in the
evening five companies of infantry charged to their rescue
amidst a storm of bullets. One company (West Riding) lost

79 men out of 100 and all but one of their officers. Of another company all their officers fell. But the charge succeeded and the Germans were again driven from Hill 60. It was sheer hand to hand fighting throughout, pressing their bayonets home like so many madmen, flinging deadly bombs into each others faces, cracking skulls with the butts of rifles. When the job was done Brigadier General O'Gowan, who directed the assault, relieved the exhausted men in the trenches by a fresh force at midnight. Fifty officers and 1500 men had fallen when General Northey took over, and the bodies of British and German lay strewn thickly over the fatal hill.

Next day and the next came a terrific bombardment, and it was noticed that some of the shells emitted a nauseous vapour which none had ever experienced before. It was a foretaste of what was to happen a few days later at the other side of the Salient. One shell blew in a parapet and buried an officer and 20 men of the Surreys. During the fighting of the 20th less than a platoon of survivors held the crest of the hill, but the young subaltern clung fast, and for his heroism that day received the Victoria Cross. Shortly after midnight every man in the detachment had been killed or wounded. A report came that the men in the advance trenches were retiring. A message was despatched to enquire if this was the case. The reply came: " We have not budged a yard and do not intend to." During this awful night of fighting, in one company of the Surreys five officers fell — two killed outright. One who survived, Lieut. Rowsall, was awarded the Cross.

Daylight came and the 1st. Devons were brought up and the fighting went on. The British death-roll was doubled. Field guns were now added to trench mortar and minenwerfers. Snipers concealed on their stomachs in shell-holes took terrible toll. But the end of the five days struggle was at hand. Our own field guns were dragged up and replied with such deadly effect that the German ones were silenced.

5

Our men rallied in force, drove out the lurking enemy and at last the victory was ours. Hill 60 remained one of the fiercest — if not the very fiercest — battle of the War. As Conan Doyle says :

" Hill 60 was a secondary matter. What was really being fought for was the ascendancy of the British over the Prussian soldier — that subtle thing which would tinge every battle which might be fought thereafter. "

Our victory, even at so terrible a cost, supplied the answer.

On Thursday, April 22nd. 1915, throughout the morning and early afternoon apart from the long distance shelling of Ypres and a bombardment of part of the line held by the Canadian 2nd. Brigade, conditions might have seemed normal. But they were not normal. There was everywhere, even amongst the civilians, a feeling of apprehension. A suspicious movement of troops and transport behind the enemy's line was reported and an attack was to be expected in this sector. But of the nature of this attack no one dreamed. At this season of the year the wind, usually from the west and north-west veered frequently to the south. But no one had ever given much thought to the wind as a dangerous element in land battle. It was now to prove vital; for at this moment the preparations of the enemy were complete and the conditions were judged favorable for the introduction of asphyxiating gas, a new and diabolical device of modern warfare.

The apparatus containing this gas, as well as asphyxiating grenades, bombs and shells, were brought up on the 18th. and distributed amongst the troops facing the troops of the French 45th. Colonial Division, the attack being timed for the 20th. In the selection of this particular sector the Germans showed great cunning. Upon no soldiers would such a device work a more paralyzing effect than upon the Zouaves, Turcos and Spahis of the Algerian desert, who gallant warriors as they are, are superstitious and subject to panic. If one wonders why they were placed in this highly critical sector at all, one must consider not merely the enormous length of line held by the French, and the arrangement by which the British were to take over the Northern sectors, but also the fact that nothing crucial was expected here. Even the placing of the Canadians in this sector was in the nature of an experiment. Even after the First Battle of Ypres, the Higher Command did not seem fully to realise that here was the Allies' most vital part : that if Ypres were over-run there would be nothing to prevent the onrush to continue until Northern Flanders and Dunkirk and Calais were in possession of the enemy, from whence they would have England at the mercy of their guns.

At 4.45 the signal was given by the enemy, whose troops were in readiness to advance, to release the gas. A few minutes later a cloud of poisonous vapour was rolling swiftly before the wind from their trenches, running almost due east and west, between a point north of Langemarck-Steenstraat on the Ypres Canal.

At this moment of the afternoon, General Alderson was with the artillery commander, Colonel Morrison, at a point north east of St. Julien inspecting the position of a battery. Suddenly heavy rifle fire on the right of the French line was heard.

" Directly afterwards, " he states, " two clouds of yellowish green smoke appeared. These clouds spread rapidly, literally until they appeared to merge into each other. It was evident from the nearing sound of their rifle fire that the Germans were advancing rapidly behind the clouds. "

The General instantly divined that some devilry was afoot and that no time was to be lost to cope with it. He and his companion had left their horses at Wieltje and they hurried back thither in order to avoid being cut off. As they passed through the batteries south east of FORTUIN, they heard the order " Stand to, " being shouted. By the time they got to Wieltje village they saw a panic stricken

rabble of Turcos and Zouaves with grey faces and protruding
eyeballs, clutching their throats and choking as they ran,
many of them dropping in their tracks and lying on the
sodden earth with limbs convulsed and features distorted in
death. On, on they ran, these wretches, across the Canal to
BRIELEN and VLAMERTINGHE, some entering Ypres
by the Dixmude Gate, startling our soldiers and the lingering
remnant of the civil population.

The trenches manned by the French Colonials were thus
being abandoned pell-mell. The French line had given way.
The question was, how far had the disaster gone — could
the rout be checked ? The moment the situation was grasp-
ed by the officer commanding the 3rd. Canadian Infantry
Brigade (Brig.-General Turner) he ordered up his reserve
battalion, then at St. Julien to the rescue of the French
on his left, whose officers were doing their utmost to rally
their men by bringing fire to bear. The German attack
developed rapidly, but the smart firing held them in check
for a time, and when the Canadian improvised left gradually
gave way it was still a scene of stubborn fighting. At
night by 6.45 the Germans had pressed forward close to
St. Julien, two and a half companies defending the line
being ordered now to retire. Assistance in the shape of
reserves being urgently needed General Alderson despatched
a divisional reserve battalion, the 16th. (Canadian Highlanders) of the 3rd Brigade to General Turner, and ordered
another reserve unit, the 10th. to " stand to. "

" Guard your left, and use your brigade reserve battalion
to prevent your being turned. It is most important to maintain the high ground near your subsidiary line. "

Half an hour later (7.10 p.m.) Turner reported that he
could not stem the retirement, that ammunition was giving
out and that he had asked the Second Canadian Brigade
(General Currie) for support. Ammunition was rushed up,
but before it had arrived the German fire had slackened, and
the enemy was reported to be digging himself in. At this

juncture, the V. corps commander being appealed to, ordered up two Canadian battalions (the 2nd. and 3rd.) then forming part of the Corps reserve into the front line held by the unfortunate French victims of the gas attack.

Yet it was manifest that Turner's left flank was still more or less ' in the air.' The French General, Putz, was doing his utmost to rally his troops of the 45th. division, and prepare a counter-attack in the hope of regaining the lost trenches, and called on General Alderson to assist him. Meanwhile French troops were mixed up with the Canadian left, and while long sections of French were unmanned, others were swarming with troops of various units without direction.

A serious feature of the situation now revealed itself. In addition to the fifty odd guns which fell into the hands of the Germans on the left, four British 4.7s. forming the second London Heavy Battery which had been attached to the Canadian Division and posted behind the French, fell to the enemy. The loss of these guns made it for days impossible to reply to the enemy's heavies which he had brought down from Ostend, and which wrought much havoc among our troops.

That night (April 22nd.) witnessed wild fighting. There was a five mile breach in the British line, which if the enemy had seized his chance might well have been rushed and Ypres would surely have fallen. But he never followed up his dishonourable *coup* and the chance was for ever lost.

They might however still hope to take the Canadian 3rd. Brigade's (Turner) flank, now that it was bent back and unsupported. It was a critical moment. The 13th. battalion (Royal Highlanders of Montreal) and the 15th. (48th. High-landers) were on the exposed left of the line. To fill the gap General Turner extended his formation to the utmost, and ordered his men to shoot without ceasing as long as they had a round left. Some Canadian guns pivotted around and began sending shrapnel into the oncoming foe at a 200 yard range. Two British battalions also helped in this work. A couple of reserve battalions came hurrying up from Ypres, where the shelling continued hot, (16th. and 10th.) and set forward to the wood west of St. Julien, where the captured British guns lay. They came upon them at midnight, standing up grim and formidable in the moonlight ; but the gun-teams were miles away and there was no means of removing them. But the breech-blocks were removed and the guns made useless to the enemy. For a time the Canadians held the whole of the wood and kept the Germans at bay. In this advance Colonel Boyle (10th.) was slain and Colonel Leckie (16th.) seeing himself surrounded by the foe withdrew his men. Before dawn from all points reinforcements were on their way, but by the time they could arrive the Germans might break through. They had already captured Steenstraate, had crossed the canal, had taken LIZERNE and were on the outskirts of BOESINGHE. The Canadian 1st. Brigade (Mercer) were pushed up to counter-attack, suffering heavily. One battalion lost its commander (Col. Birchall) and stirred to anger by his death ran forward and carried the German trenches where they remained without relief for two days. But at last we were now in touch with the fast rallying French troops.

By daylight, on St. George's Day the reinforcements arrived. They were mixed battalions, hurried through the night from the British 28th. Division, which was holding the line from Zonnebeke to POLYGON WOOD, and a lot of reserve units of various regiments under Colonel Geddes of the Buffs, and now known to history as Geddes Detachment. On the way they were joined by a grenadier company of the Northumberland Fusiliers who for eight days had been in the trenches at HILL 60 and were weary and hungry, but not too weary to fight. Also General Allenby's cavalry and two Indian divisions were hastening forward to buttress the French west of the Canal.

All that day the battle continued, the brunt being borne by the Canadian 3rd. Brigade, who, half gassed, nearly exhausted, without water or proper rations, exposed to fire from three sides, hung valiantly on, or when compelled to retire, moved slowly back to St. Julien. A company of the Buffs came up to help, but it was shot to pieces. Colonel Geddes himself was killed.

Meanwhile the German heavy guns from PASSCHEN-DAELE Ridge were booming and the great shells were bursting amongst the defenders of Ypres and in the doomed town itself. The fury of the bombardment hourly increased. And in addition came a fresh discharge of poison gas. The ordeal which the troops, especially the 13th. Canadian battalion — underwent, seemed more than human endurance could bear.

By the retirement of the 3rd. Brigade upon St. Julien, the 2nd. Brigade (Currie) which had hitherto held its ground, had to conform, all except Colonel Lipsett's 8th. battalion Grafenstafel ridge, the north-eastern extremity of holding the Salient — which did not budge but although heavily gassed held fast to the line.

On the 24th. the new St. Julien line was stormed by the enemy, but with scant success ; and on Sunday the 25th. we were strong enough to undertake a general counter-attack under the command of General Hull. But although the struggle was intense we could not retake St. Julien and were obliged to dig ourselves in just south of Fortuin.

In another part of the Salient at BROODSEINDE held by the 28th. division which had furnished reserves to the Canadians, the enemy, thinking the defence thereby weakened, made a violent assault aided by gas shells. It failed.

That evening the Canadians were allowed a much needed rest. Colonel Lipsetts's 8th. Battalion (Winnipeg Rifles) had held on stubbornly to GRAFENSTAFEL for four days in spite of gas, bombs and machine-gun enfilading. At last the parapets of its trenches were blown in, filling the ditch, and the heroic fighters had perforce fallen back to Wieltje and now looked forward to repose. *

The Lahore Indian Division (Keary) came into the line, and in view of reinforcements elsewhere a general counter-attack was ordered for the 26th.. For 1500 yards the Indian troops advanced bravely and then a fresh emission of the terrible poison gas stopped them. Many perished on the spot, and the remainder, although stupefied and staggering, seized their shovels and dug themselves in. The arrangements for the attack had been made too hurriedly. We had not used our artillery enough. But the Indians had done a fine thing. To advance, as General Smith-Dorrien said, " up an open slope in the face of overwhelming shell, rifle and machine gun fire and clouds of poison gas : but " he added, " it prevented the German advance and ensured the safety of Ypres.   Several battalions had been almost wiped out — the 29th Baluchis could muster afterwards only 100 men.

On the right the trenches were held by the Northumbrian Brigade (Riddell). Its 6th. battalion managed to reach a point in the attack 250 yards beyond its starting point, but its losses were enormous. General Riddell was killed, together with 42 officers and 1800 men of his brigade, and a retirement was ordered.

At Grafenstafel the Canadians had been succeeded by the 85th. Brigade who were also compelled to yield a part of the ridge. On their right came the 26th. Division which stood firm.   Much fighting took place south-west of St. Julien (13th. Brigade) at the Vanheule farm (which our men called Shell-trap Farm) and for the next few days the struggle went on in all parts of the line. On May 1st. a desperate bombardment took place between Grafenstafel and Zonnebeke.

It was now decided that the Ypres Salient was far too

* " If the Salient of Ypres will be for all time the classic battle-ground of Britain, that blood-stained segment between the Poelcapelle and Zonnebeke roads will remain the holy land of Canadian arms. " *Buchan.* This was written in 1916 before Sanctuary Wood and Passchendaele.

broad a battle-field to be held against such artillery and overwhelming forces. The German attack on May 2nd. a bloody
affair between the Ypres Canal and Fortuin, assisted by
gas, confirmed the decision.   On the following day it was
carried out methodically.   The wounded had to be moved
out from the field hospitals, the supplies and ammunition, and
then the trenches were silently evacuated, without the loss of
a man or a gun.   The retirement affected the British right
and made the Salient a curve whose apex was less than three
miles from Ypres. Abandoning GRAVENSTAFEL and ZON-
NEBEKE, just taking in FREZENBERG and HOOGHE.
From thence it curved round to the ZILLEBEKE rigde
and HILL 60.

It was on the 5th. of May that HILL 60 fell to the Germans.

For it was not in flesh and blood to withstand such a
devilish contrivance as asphyxiating gas.   We had not then
devised either a protection or antidote.   Hill 60 was therefore
to witness a further deadly struggle, in which the valour of
our troops could not count against the vapours of hell.   On
May 1st the Germans released gas in enormous quantities.
The fumes enveloped the summit of the hill, guarded by the
Dorsets, who were strangled by the gas where they lay.
So thick and penetrating was the green cloud that the
Germans themselves could not approach, and it was the
relieving battalions of Devons and Bedfords who first penetrated to the trenches on the summit, only to find the dead
bodies of their comrades and the survivors writing in agony.

Foiled this time, the enemy repeated his attempt on May
5th, gassing the 2nd West Ridings (The Duke's).

" There appeared, staggering towards the dug-out of the
commanding officer of the Duke's in the rear two figures,
an officer and an orderly.   The officer was pale as death and
when he spoke his voice came hoarsely from his throat.
Beside him his orderly, with unbuttoned coat, his rifle clasped
in his hand, swayed as he stood.   The officer said slowly, in
his gasping voice: ' They have gassed the Duke's.   I believe

I was the last man to leave the hill. The men up there are
all dead. They were splendid. I thought I ought to come
and report.' ' That officer was Captain Robins..... They took
him and his faithful orderly to hospital, but the gallant officer
died that night. His two subalterns, Lieut. Miller and
another, both remained in the front trench until they died. "

(Valentine Williams)

The Germans at last gained the crest of Hill 60, while the
British clung to the sides nearest our line. But there was
now little left of the hill, which had been mined and shelled out
of all recognition, so that the peasantry who came back to see
it after the war could hardly distinguish the site. And to-day
many visitors confound the eminence on the other side of the
railway (" The Dump ") with the immortal Hill 60. On May
8th. an enemy attack was made on the centre of our line,
held by the 28th. Division, which pushed us back west of
FREZENBERG ridge, a battle which inflicted terrible losses
on the 1st. Suffolks, the 2nd. Cheshires and other regiments.
The only battalion which kept their ground was the first
Welsh, who stayed until they were ordered to retire. The
falling back of the 83rd. Brigade left their neighbours on the
right exposed. These were the Canadian Princess Patricias,
who fought like heroes this day. All the senior officers,
(including Major Hamilton Gault) were either killed or
wounded, so that the command devolved upon Lieutenant
Hugh Niven, who had joined up as a private and retired
three years later as a field officer. The trenches of the
Patricias were demolished and the troops manned the communication trench and continued the fight until late that
night when, their strength and ammunition spent, they were
relieved. At the roll-call only 150 out of 700 responded.

The same day (8th.) saw the 4th. Division attacked in
force. The German losses were very great. WIELTJE
was captured and then retaken by us. But the net result
was that the Salient was still further lessened. May 9th.
saw hot fighting on and about the Menin Road and the north

of BELLEWAARDE lake ; and these attacks were resumed
on the 10th. when the garrison of many British trenches was
annihilated, the Camerons, and Argyll and Sutherland High-
landers suffering heavily. Still the Germans slowly crept on
towards Ypres, and it became necessary for the V. Corps
commander (Plumer) to use up his valuable cavalry in the
depleted trenches. It seemed a dangerous and a desperate
measure ; but it was necessary. So De Lisle's force (1st. and
3rd. Cavalry Division) were put in, in the hope that the German
force was now nearly spent. Scarce had the dismounted
troopers gone in, on a day of storm of rain, as well as steel,
than a murderous bombardement lasting 14 hours broke out
to the north of the YPRES-ROULERS road. The cavalry
and yeomanry met the shock with set teeth. Of one regiment the commander in chief reported :

" The North Somerset Yeomanry on the right of the brigade, (7th.) although also suffering severely hung on in their
trenches throughout the day, and actually advanced and
attacked the enemy with the bayonet. These were the men
whom the Germans believed they had blown into the air. "

The 18th. Hussars at Wieltje lost 150 men out of their
thinned ranks. The line of the Salient was again dented
towards the middle, but to the north and south held firm.
The battle was now all but over, and on the 13th. May the
German attempt to capture Ypres had once more ended in
costly failure.

It was on the 13th. that the 10th. Hussars and the Blues
sprang forward to fill a gap made by the retirement of the
7th. Brigade which endured a living hell until the human
frame and nerves threatened to collapse. They were assisted
by a detachment of armoured motor-cars commanded by the
Duke of Westminster, which showed their value this day, and
this charge of dismounted cavalry will for ever find a place
in history. The 3rd. Cavalry Division had fought only a
single day and lost 91 officers and 1050 men.

Had the Germans gone on, none may tell what might have

happened — a heap of British corpses would perhaps alone
have barred the way to Ypres and Calais. But their
store of ammunition — vast as it was — was spent, and the
gas cylinders were empty. It took 10 days to replenish the
latter and on May 24th. in the early morning, a bank of
green vapour, three miles long, came floating with the breeze
towards the British trenches between Shell-trap Farm and
BELLEWAARDE LAKE. The cloud was 40 feet in height.
This time the intended victims, the troops of the 4th. Division, had some protection in the shape of respirators, but the
surprise was in many instances so great that large numbers were
gassed out of action. On the heels of the gas came a violent
shelling which made our men recoil a little, especially about
Shell-trap Farm and near the Menin Road. But a strong counter-attack blew the Germans back to their trenches " like
rabbits" as one Essex officer wrote. The fight was distinguished
by the steadfast behaviour of the cavalry, who lost this day a
splendid leader in Captain Francis Grenfell V. C., whose
memory will ever be cherished in the annals of British arms.

The result of the latest fighting was that the Germans
had captured Bellewaarde Lake, and our new line ran
from the west of it to Hooghe. A week after the terrific
fighting just recorded, this same Hooghe, chateau and
village, were first bombarded, and then rushed by the enemy's
troops. It was a local action like that at Hill 60, and the
3rd. Dragoon Guards held the line until June 3rd. until they
were nearly destroyed, and of Hooghe only the site remained.

The British losses were 100.000 men in The Second
Ypres Battle ; that of the Germans was at least double.
The result was only to show that the German machine was
superior to ours and that our men were superior to a machine.
Wherever we had got to grips with the enemy we had
worsted him, and his reliance upon such dastardly methods
of war as poison gas covered the German name throughout the world with obloquy. And as the attempt proved
it was even worse than a crime — it was a blunder.

THE BATTLE OF SANCTUARY WOOD

Following the SECOND BATTLE OF YPRES the fighting in the Salient continued to be of a desultory kind, for the Germans, despairing of immediate success in breaking the Allied line turned their attention elsewhere, especially to the Russian campaign. The British line extended as far north as Boesinghe, where were the VI. Corps (Keir) V. Corps (Allenby) — these to the north of Hooghe. To the south of Hooghe was the II. Corps (Ferguson) and the III. Corps (Pulteney).

On June 16th. there occurred a smart action just north of Hooghe. An officer of the 9th. Brigade which went forward through Ypres to the fighting line, wrote : " The sight of the ruined beauties of that once glorious old town, did lots to make us long to get at the Vandals who had done this wanton act of destruction." All through the war the same feeling was evoked among our troops by the spectacle of Ypres.

The fighting about Hooghe went on with great fierceness during June, July and part of August — when the names of BELLEWAARDE, ZOUAVE WOOD, and the Moated Grange were on everybody's lips.

Then in September the scene shifted southward to LOOS, where a terrific battle was fought, and later, in March 1916, to NEUVE CHAPELLE.

Meanwhile trench warfare went on in the Salient, accompanied by a constant bombardment. At ST. ELOI the enemy again tried to enter, and the fighting there cost both sides heavily.

But the Salient was held fast — more and more was it consecrated by heroic deeds.

" When, " wrote a gifted English chronicler, " the war is over, this triangle of meadowland with a ruined city for its base, will be an enclave of Belgian soil consecrated as the holy land of two great peoples. It may be that it will be

specially set apart as a memorial place ; it may be that it will
be unmarked, and that the countryfolk will till and reap as
before, over the vanishing trench lines. But it will never be
common ground. It will be for us the most hallowed spot
on earth, for it holds our bravest dust, and it is the proof and
record of a new spirit. In the past when we have thought
of Ypres, we have thought of the British flag preserved
there, which Clare's Regiment, fighting for France, captured
at the battle of Ramillies, the name of the little Flemish town
has recalled the divisions in our own race and the centuries-
old conflict between France and Britain. But from now and
henceforth it will have other memories. It will stand as a
symbol of unity and alliance, unity within our Empire. unity
within our Western civilisation, that true alliance and that
lasting unity which are won and sealed by a common
sacrifice. "

Once again, foiled in his designs on Verdun, that great
battlefield of the war, the enemy, perhaps for the last time,
sought to wrest this famous ground, the Ypres Salient and
Ypres itself from our hands. This time the Canadians had
three divisions in the fighting line. The Corps commander
on the 2nd of June when the German fury burst forth anew,
was that same General Sir Julian Byng who had first, in
October 1914, at the head of his cavalry troops, marked out
the frontiers of the Salient.

This battle, began on June 2nd. At 6.30 a.m. Major General
Mercer (3rd. Division) went forward to the front trenches on
his normal tour of inspection. He was met by Brigadier
General Victor Williams, commanding the brigade then
holding the front line, and Colonel Shaw.

The soil hereabouts was loose, damp and sandy and only
by rigid care and incessant exertions could the trenches be
maintained in effectiveness. General Mercer entered a
number of the observation stations and officers' dug-outs and
examined machine-gun emplacements with care. The day's
work had begun well—all were at their appointed posts.

Occasionally a sniper's rifle rang out or a shrapnel shell burst harmlessly overhead.

It was the usual lull before the storm. For at ten minutes to nine o'clock without any warning hell broke loose. The detonation from being stunning grew absolutely overwhelming. It did not come from one part, but from the whole length of the opposing line opposite the Canadian Third Division. For the next hour or two, dazed men groped about in the storm, unable to hear any word of command from their officers, clutching their rifles, trying to save the surrounding earth from engulphing them, waiting for what was to happen. The two generals attempting to reach the communication trench found their retreat cut off.

At the outset its appears that no shells, or very few, fell into the front trenches and the machine gunners and trench-mortar men held to their posts. But behind our front line a high wall of descending steel, screaming, crashing, exploding, emitting clouds of noxious smoke, shut off chance of escape by the communication trenches and all hope of support and succour from the reserve trenches in the rear. Moments passed that seemed hours and then the iron and steel missiles began to rain down and explode in the front line, scattering death and destruction. Nothing could live for long in such a tempest. The sides of the trenches began to crumble and fall in. Yet by a miracle our men held on, darting from one devastated section to another for refuge.

Beginning with HOOGHE, which was held —600 yards of front — by the men of the Royal Canadian Regiment, there came a fifty yards gap in the line, low-lying sodden ground which was undefended — it being thought it might prove a trap for the Germans ; then came the section of front held by the Princess Patricias, which included the embowed hollow known as the 'Appendix' (only forty yards from the German trenches) and the Loop. On their right were the Canadian Mounted Rifles, who defended a portion of SANCTUARY WOOD and ARMAGH WOOD.

In the fatal Loop was stationed a whole company of the Princess Patricias. As the men hung on there, grim and expectant, there was a terrific explosion ; when the flying fragments had subsided a watcher from a balloon would have seen only a jagged and enormous crater — awful in its stillness. The Loop had been mined by the enemy and the entire company of brave men had perished. Another monstrous German mine exploded, but with less deadly effect.

By this time all the communication trenches were battered flat. Orders had somehow been conveyed to the troops to flee for their lives, and some few hundreds attempted to beat a retreat through the deadly barrage. Only a handful of them got through. The majority of the survivors stayed on the ground or hid in such refuge as they could find.

Meanwhile, on the other side of the barrage, two battalions of desperate men were watching for a chance to cleave their way through to their comrades in peril. But there was little hope that any in the front line of trenches survived.

By this time — it was ten minutes to one o'clock.—after four hours steady bombardment — the storm of shell ceased as suddenly as it had begun. Forthright from the opposite trenches sprang a swarm of grey-coated Huns. Fully accoutred and with overcoats and full haversacks they advanced on the run, yelling wildly. They must have been firmly convinced that amidst those rugged, battered, seared and bloody mounds and ditches, which four hours before had been the British trenches, not one single soul had escaped. For, apart from a few bombers, not a man of those advancing hordes appears to have been in proper fighting trim. They came forward gaily, light-heartedly, as victors after a victory.

It was then the most wonderful thing of the day happened. Out of the earth there sprang up a handful of wild-eyed soldiers, two officers amongst them, muddied and reeking with sweat, and running forward, with upraised rifles and pistols, bade defiance to the oncoming foe. On they ran and having discharged their weapons, flung them in the very faces of the Huns. Death was inevitable for these — the only surviving occupants of the British front line and it was better to die thus, breathing defiance to a cowardly enemy, than be shot in a ditch and spitted through with a Hun bayonet.

Few but the wounded fell into the hands of the enemy. A Toronto Officer, himself in the very thick of the fight and performing wonders of valour, told me that he had last seen General Mercer sitting dazed and wounded on the ground, just as the shell-fire ceased and the Germans were advancing. Amongst the prisoners were General Williams and Colonel Usher, both of whom were lying in a communication trench at "Vigo Street". General Williams was wounded in the face.

The cessation of fire was the signal for the Canadian supports to hasten forward to meet the enemy, who was now advancing in force, and bringing up his machine-gunners and bombers. The battalion holding Maple Copse became planted firmly and refused to budge, and having dug itself in, held that position all day. Colonel Baker, of the Mounted Rifles, was unhappily hit by a shell in the lungs and died later in the day. The Princess Patricias fought with all their accustomed gallantry led by the brave Colonel Buller, and helped, although at great cost, to check the further German advance.

Buller, his blood up, seeing his men giving way a little, ordered them to charge along a trench known as Gordon Road. He was encouraging them when he was slain. The second in command of the Patricias, Major Hamilton Gault, was severly wounded.

The machine guns of the Royal Canadian Regiment inflicted fearful mortality. Between them and the Princess Patricias was a gap, fifty yards wide, into which the Germans poured on finding it undefended, and were smashed on both flanks, being mowed down by scores. On their arrival at the " Appendix " only forty yards from the enemy's front trenches, they were met by a withering fire which almost obliter-

6

ated them.   A little further south, they were more successful,
and from the "Loop" where an entire company of the Princess
Patricias had perished, they penetrated to Gordon Road and
beyond and then commenced a fierce attack to the north.
But here a swift and stern retribution was to be exacted from
them.   A company commander, Captain Hugh Niven who,
although already twice wounded, was still full of valour and
resolution, gathered the remainder of his company together,
some seventy rifles in all and two machine guns, and hidden
behind sandbags awaited the foe in silence.   The order was
given. " Not a man must shoot until I give " the signal ! "
Apparently, the Boche was taken unawares.   The volley
which blazed forth was reminiscent of the immortal front
rank fire of Lascelle's Regiment at Quebec.   One stalwart
French-Canadian, Arsenault by name, who had often faced
wild animals in the backwoods, burning with ardour, could
not be restrained from leaping up on the improvised parapet
and repeatedly emptying his rifle, before the enemy could recover from his astonishment. His captain related that no fewer
than eight Germans fell to this man's marksmanship alone in
that swift encounter.   When it was over, at least a hundred
of the enemy slain lay on the ground.   Afterwards the officer
mentioned shepherded his men into a section of trench, he
himself spending the whole of the ensuing night perambulat-
ing the trenches directing defences, ministering to and
encouraging and directing his men.

On the edge of the craters the bodies were seen of a stalwart Sergeant Major of the Mounted Rifles and two privates
of the Princess Patricias.   Lying around and beneath them,
were the bodies of twelve of the enemy, whom they had
slain by the bayonet.

By half-past five o'clock the enemy had penetrated and
possessed themselves of about a mile of our front line
trenches, in the middle of the arc they had attacked with
such demoniac force.   The trenches south of HOOGHE for
1000 yards we still held and also the front east of HILL 60.

After nightfall the Germans pushed on 700 yards further towards ZILLEBEKE and proceeded to entrench themselves firmly. For the moment their artillery had won them an advantage, but the price they had paid was at least as terrible as our own.

That night while the enemy was preparing to hold his new front and the stretcher-bearers and Red Cross workers on both sides were bringing in their wounded and dead, General Sir Julian Byng, the Corps Commander, was planning the counter-attack to recover the ground which had been lost. This attack was delayed for some hours, owing to the necessity for assembling artillery in such force as to silence the enemy, who still kept up a vigorous bombardment, occasionally becoming intense.

The advance was timed for six o'clock in the morning, but still the barrage did not lift and it was nearly half-past nine when our troops moved forward in earnest. These troops belonged to the First and Third Divisions, but the brunt of the fighting was borne by survivors of the 7th and 8th brigades of the latter division, assisted by two companies of the King's Royal Rifles, an Imperial regiment which had been serving in the Salient.

A bombardment of a vigour almost equal to that of the Germans of the previous day created a shelter for our advancing battalions. The enemy guns replied, and at one time the spectacle was witnessed of a double barrage of appalling intensity. None the less, the Canadians pushed on, and after fighting all day succeeded in reaching a portion of their old front-line trenches in the northern section. On the way thither they came across numbers of enemy dead lying about unburied. The trenches were however battered to pieces and they were not in sufficient strength to hold on. The same was true of the battalions of the 8th Brigade who advanced south of Maple Copse and east of Warrington Avenue, although the 49th batallion, which had lost its commanding officer, Col. Baker, M.P., struggled valiantly for a time to maintain itself. The result was that we were forced back to a new front line of trenches near ZILLEBEKE.

The losses of these two days had been grievous — some 7.000 killed and wounded. General Mercer, had fallen. Just as the Huns were making their advance at half-past one o'clock the General was seen supporting himself against a parapet at the entrance of a dug-out known as the Tube, suffering from shell shock and there beyond doubt he met his death. A brigade commander and a battalion commander were taken prisoners. Two other colonels, Buller and Baker, had been slain.

The Battle of Sanctuary Wood illustrated vividly the whole character of the fighting in the war. It combined the essential features of all, with the exception of poison gas. Brief, compact and murderous, it was by far the greatest artillery ordeal to which the Canadians had yet been subjected. As an exhibition of German frightfulness on the one hand and British steadfastness on the other, it is unsurpassed in the war.

The earth was all torn, seared and fretted hereabouts, but a surprising amount of fine timber still stood. All through those two fierce days' fighting, wounded men were crawling about or lying motionless for hours either helpless or to avoid observation. One man spent two nights on his back in No Man's Land without food, drink or succour. Another was thrice buried by the effects of the much-vaunted minenwerfer shell, which ploughs up the surrounding earth, and thrice dug out by a passing officer. Machine guns were repeatedly buried and then rapidly and diligently excavated and brought again into action, much to the enemy's amazement and discomfiture.

On June 13th. the Canadian troops, chafing over the results of the fierce German offensive of the past ten days, planned and successfully carried through in the early hours of a counter-attack which restored every foot of valuable ground they had lost,—OBSERVATORY RIDGE, the whole of Armagh

Wood and the uplands to the south including Mount Sorel.

The night was wet, cold and thoroughly disagreeable, but the men were in the highest possible spirits at the prospect of an advance to recover their old position. This time our artillery was fully prepared and at 1.30 o'clock in the morning, under cover of a heavy fire, the advance began. A fresh Canadian division had been sent into the Salient and there remained a mixed brigade of those Canadian mounted troops who figured in the previous fighting. General Lipsett, succeeding General Mercer, deferred taking up his command in order to lead his old brigade into action.

To three battalions the attack was mainly entrusted. A fourth battalion to the right, opposite HILL 60 provided a diversion for the enemy, so as to prevent the attacking battalions from being enfiladed, while on the extreme left where there was less ground to be retaken, a fifth battalion advanced. The orders were to take three lines of trenches and to establish bomb posts in the fourth.

These four trenches were (1) the new German front line which they had recently made, (2) our old reserve trench, (3) our old support trench, and (4) our old front line.

The troops pressed forward, the Germans falling back sullenly under the impetuosity of the attack. Some fierce fighting took place here and there in the territory south of Warrington Avenue, especially for the possession of Observatory Ridge, but the enemy seemed helpless before the fury of our impetus. Early in the engagement two of his guns mounted on his ground south of the famous " Appendix " fell into our hands.

Trench after trench was re-taken, the Canadians sending up a mighty cheer when they discovered that a great quantity of stores which they had left there ten days before, half-buried by the force of minenwerfer shells, had been undiscovered or at least unremoved by the enemy and were practically intact. Three German officers and 140 men were made prisoners.

The supporting battalions came through the deadly barrage at last and went to the relief of those which had spent the whole of Tuesday in constant fighting. " It was a " magnificent thing " one officer told me, " to watch those " fellows pushing in past three barrages, many of them hit " and stopping awhile to bind up their wounds, and then " up and at it again, like dare-devils that nothing could baulk. " I have never seen anything finer. "

Once the relieving force was in the recovered British trenches, the bombardment of the latter grew very hot and in those sections of the line where our old outposts had not been reached, much desperate fighting took place in the ensuing forty-eight hours; the tide of battle flowing this way or that, as a hill or trench was taken by us or re-taken by the enemy. One officer on the first day had advanced his machine gun in a favourable position to prevent enfilading, in case the Germans should return to this particular trench. The Germans did return, a shell lifted the gun clean out over the officer's head and he lay stunned for a while on the ground. When he recovered consciousness, the Germans were behind him ; in a moment with little assistance he had it working briskly in the opposite direction and was hard at it, when a shell gave him a mortal wound.

Forty-eight hours after the relieving battalions went in they in turn were relieved. For two days and two nights they had been subjected to a terrific hammering, and few of either officers or men had had a moment's sleep. When the respite came many of them on the way back sank down in the mud of what three days' before had been No Man's Land and slept peacefully, utterly worn out. Several told me that when they awoke, it was to find an equally exhausted slumbering Boche a few paces away. These stragglers continue to come in, some of them wholly unwounded, having been for days wandering about, virtually without food, and drinking only such water as they find in the rain-drenched ditches.

Such was the battle of Sanctuary Wood, where the Canadians added another glorious chapter to their military history.

THE THIRD BATTLE OF

YPRES

On June 7th. 1917, by the capture of MESSINES and
WYTSCHAETE the British Commander-in-Chief, Sir Douglas
Haig, began what was destined to become the long series of
engagements which history will know as the THIRD BATTLE
OF YPRES. Having now got into his possession the high
ground to the south of the Salient the Field Marshal turned
his attention to the half circle of hills around YPRES which
in successive waves rise to the height of PASSCHEN-
DAELE, and from whence the enemy who held all these
heights could command the whole Salient. These von Arnim
the German commander was resolved not to yield ; so while
the British army was winning its way elsewhere he had
proceeded to construct a formidable barrier to any British
advance in this quarter. Still hoping to break through at
YPRES, he had gone on nibbling at the Salient ever since
the Second Battle of YPRES, until his troops were established hardly further than two miles from the town. HOOGHE
was in his hands with the BELLEWAARDE Farm.

Yet von Arnim was still playing a defensive game : he
knew the British would soon concentrate themselves for the
capture of NIEUPORT, OSTEND, BRUGES and the
Belgian coast, where the submarine bases were and they
must be checked.

Owing to the myriad shell-holes and the sodden condition
of the intervening ground, it was impossible to construct
another Siegfried line of deep dug-outs and concrete lined
trenches. He therefore had recourse to the "pill-boxes".

These were small concrete forts partially sunk in the soil and
heavily armed, containing 20 to 40 men with machine guns ;
many examples of which can still be seen dotting the Salient.

But besides their great strength in proportion to their
size the pill-boxes possessed the inestimable advantage of
being capable of rapid construction. It was only necessary
to set up the steel frame work during the night, and fill it up

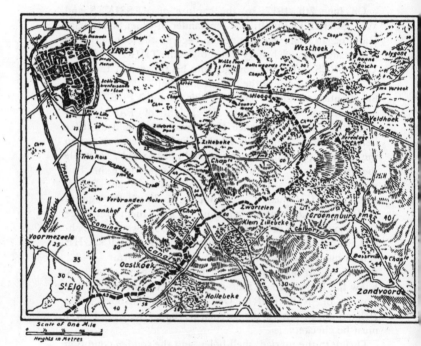

THIRD BATTLE OF YPRES

with concrete three feet thick. Moreover they were thus
invulnerable to field guns, and, owing to their small size, a
bad target for heavy artillery.

June was a terrible month for Ypres in the throes of the German bombardment.

Throughout July a fierce British artillery fire spread further ruin and desolation, if that were possible, over the northern and eastern extremities of the Salient, in preparation for the coming great battle. This tempest of steel was accompanied by constant infantry raids and gas attacks. One of the most deadly of the latter took place in almost exactly the spot (St. Julien) where this hellish invention had first been tried by the Germans in the Second Battle of Ypres along the Passchendaele Road. This time it was he who was the sufferer.

On the 27th. July it was found that the enemy had suddenly fallen back from his trenches near Boesinghe where Gough's 5th. Army joined up with the French under General Anthoine. In consequence the Allies crossed the canal and manned the late German front to a length of 3000 yards, throwing over at night no fewer than 17 bridges over the canal.

On the last day of July in wretched weather, from the southermost edge of the Salient to the sea at Nieuport at 5.50 in the morning hell burst forth in the shape of the biggest barrage the Allies had ever launched. Over the parapets went the Allied Infantry and back went the Germans. Like an expanding wave on the waters, so swelled the line of the Salient. HOLLEBEKE, then ZILLEBEKE, SANCTUARY WOOD and SHREWSBURY FOREST, HOOGHE, BELLEWAARDE LAKE, WESTHOEK, FRE-ZENBERG, ST. JULIEN, PILKEM, and BIXSCHOOTE. The German first line was over-run everywhere, the second line in parts. No longer could the enemy overlook the Salient. 6000 prisoners were taken, including 133 officers.

But there we stopped. The enemy had massed himself in GLENCORSE WOOD and INVERNESS COPSE — the key to his position, and on the afternoon of August 1st. the rain began to descend. For four days and nights it continued without intermission.   The surface of the land became impassible.

" The low-lying, clayey soil, torn by shells and sodden by rain, turned to a succession of vast muddy pools.   The valleys of the choked and overflowing streams were speedily transformed into long stretches of bog, impassible except by a few well-defined tracks, which became marks for the enemy's artillery.   To leave these tracks was to risk death by drowning, and in the course of the subsequent fighting on several occasions both men and pack animals were lost in this way. In these conditions operations of any magnitude became impossible, and the resumption of our offensive was necessarily postponed until a period of fine weather should allow the ground to recover.   As had been the case in the ARRAS battle, this unavoidable delay in the development of our offensive was of the greatest service to the enemy.   Valuable time was lost, the troops opposed to us were able to recover from the disorganisation produced by our first attack, and the enemy was given the opportunity to bring up reinforcement ".

(*Sir Douglas Haig's Despatch*).

Under such circumstances some withdrawals were inevitable.   ST. JULIEN had to be given up for a few days, but by the 16th., although the weather was not yet settled, the advance was resumed.   Our attack was now directed to the German third position on the GHELUVELT-LANGE-MARCK line, north of the MENIN Road, the second tier of ridges, bordering the Salient on the east.   The third tier was PASSCHENDAELE, which must have seemed to the enemy impregnable.   von Arnim more than ever pinned his faith to his pill-boxes and his new system of ' elastic defence '.   This was officially described as one " in which his forward trench lines were held only in sufficient strength to disorganize the attack while the bulk of his force were kept in close reserve, ready to deliver a powerful and immediate blow which might recover the positions overrun by our troops, before the British had time to consolidate them. "

That day the Allies pushed on beyond the BIXSCHOOTE-

LANGEMARCK road by dint of hard fighting and took the
German third line north of LANGEMARCK. But north
and north east of ST-JULIEN, between the WIELTJE-
PASSCHENDAELE and YPRES-ZONNEBEKE roads all
their valour was bruised in vain in that terrible sea of mud.
From the innumerable pill-boxes poured a steady fire and
although we made captures, the days gains were far less than
had been hoped. The same terrible tale of fighting against
odds and ultimate failure was true of the Menin Road
advance. The troops had passed the highground (Hill 64)
but the Wood of HERENTHAGE (INVERNESS COPSE)
towards GHELUVELT, GLENCORSE WOOD and POL-
YGON WOOD (where a race-course had formerly stood)
brought them to a stand-still. On the whole field, however,
two thousand prisoners had been taken and 30 guns and we
had seriously dented the German third line.

In spite of appalling weather conditions, fighting went on
for the rest of the month. Tanks were brought in by
hundreds to assist the ill-starred 5th. Army, and scores of
them sank in the mud. Splendid troops were sacrified in
vain. von Arnim's scheme held good. A new move was
necessary, new strategy, new tactical dispositions, new
troops, and above all, as our soldiers remarked grimly, new
weather.

To the magnificent 2nd. Army under Sir Herbert Plumer
now fell the task of dislodging the Hun from the Salient.
After a few weeks of comparative quiet the attack was renewed on Sept. 19th. and the land, now partly dried about ZON-
NEBEKE, ST. JULIEN, GHELUVELT, and VELTHOEK
became again a welter of blood. The Australians fought like
heroes, capturing POLYGON WOOD, and the whole line
began to move forward through the Slough of Despond.
Smarting under his losses of 3000 Germans von Arnim
launched next day 11 cannon attacks. For nearly a week the
British fought their ground inch by inch, while the enemy
mediatated a monster counter-attack, before we could set foot

on the slopes of PASSCHENDAELE. It was necessary to act quickly. On Oct. 4th. was anticipated his advance by only 10 minutes, and our barrage dealt havoc to his formations. We got into POELCAPELLE, GRAFENSTAFEL and BROODSEINDE, passing beyond the BECELARE road. 5000 prisoners fell to us that day. It was a victory, but at what a price ! and how below our hopes ! There had been 10 weeks of fighting, and all that we had accomplished we had planned to perform in a single fortnight. We had not won even the preliminary objective of July 3rd. — the PASSCHENDAELE RIDGE. Winter was coming on, and the enemy still held the high ground. For a time Haig hesitated whether or not to abandon the offensive. Then he decided to continue it until the end of the month. If PASSCHENDAELE was then uncaptured, other plans must be made.

No wonder, then, that the whole army and the nation concentrated its attention eagerly on this famous ridge.

On Oct. 9th. a new Franco-British advance was begun with the rain falling in sheets. For the rest of the month the Salient was a greater sea of mud than it had ever been in the war. Never — scarce even in the winter of 1914-15 — had the troops fought under such wretched conditions. On — — with men staggering under the burden — and they and their horses drowning by scores and hundreds in the slime — on they pushed, each day a little further.

If was at this juncture that the Canadian Corps was summoned from Lens. The 3rd. and 4th. Divisions, under Generals Lipsett and Watson, took over part of the line on the 20th.

The Corps Commander (General Sir Arthur Currie) realised the desperate nature of the task confronting him. The first thing was to contrive some means of transit for guns, shells and material. Thousands of men were set to work making roads across the bog, flinging down iron, steel, canarets, sandbags, tree stumps and laying a double line of planks

across. Somehow, day and night the work went on, under
the enemy gun fire; the roads were laid down, the light railway was exhumed, repaired and extended and supplies were
rushed up. Guns were laid on sandbags in shell holes, and
even then many sank and were lost. A rather disastrous
feature was the German's temporary superiority in air-craft
which caused the Canadians to be bombed, even in broad
daylight as never before. In a single night 1000 bombs were
dropped in and around Ypres. The 4th. Canadian Division
Headquarters were at the Menin Gate and from the
ramparts there the divisional commander could watch the
action of the artillery during that critical time.

The October weather continued atrocious. In the British
trenches it passed into a proverb : " *The weather is always
Boche.* " Even when the sun shone it seemed to be in
irony ; for the vast watery plain yielded up none of its
moisture. On October 22nd. the British advanced east of
POELCAPELLE further into the HOUTHULST FOREST
and four days later (Friday the 26th.) the Canadians were
ordered to attack between the ROULERS railway and
POELCAPELLE. From PASSCHENDAELE two elevat-
ions ran westward, called the BELLEVUE SPUR and the
GRAFENSTAFEL SPUR. Between these two ridges
courses a tiny stream called the Ravebeck. Along the banks
of his stream the Canadians moved against the PAS-
SCHENDAELE RIDGE. On the Bellevue Spur the old
German front line trenches ran and the fighting here was
heavy. Just below the crest of the hill was a row of three
concrete " pill-boxes ". These were rapidly taken by assault,
the troops stumbling over the dead bodies of the enemy slain
by our artillery. Word then came that the Ontario troops
moving on Dad trench had been forced back after hand-to-
hand fighting. One officer, Lieut. Clarke, who had gained
the trench stuck to it and actually made 63 Germans
prisoners. But this local retirement necessitated a readjustment of the line. The Canadian Mounted Rifles were in a

critical position, and elsewhere the mud had jammed rifles and machine guns.

At this juncture, when a general retirement seemed imminent, a party of 20 Canadian Cameronians gained the summit on the left of the BELLEVUE Spur from whence they could command a view of the surrounding country. While they rested for a moment in disorder, and many of them wounded they were rallied by Lieut. Shankland, who secured reinforcements and proceeded to clear the whole precints of the enemy. For four hours they held on, resisting every attempt at dislodgment, and then Shankland, although wounded, hurried back to report to his commander :

" I have 50 men on top of the ridge. We command the entire position. Give me reinforcements and the hill is ours."

Instantly the advance was renewed. Two battalions moved on Dad trench and another force went to the defence of BELLEVUE SPUR. " The Canadians, " wrote an observer, " had almost to dig the enemy out of their emplacements, so firmly were they planted in. " Yet before night fell, the first day's objective was taken — nearly 1000 yards inside the German front line. Bellevue Spur was ours, and for his share in the day work Shankland received the V.C.

On the Canadian right British troops got into GHELU-VELT for the first time since the First Battle of Ypres, three years before. On the left, the 63rd. (Royal, Naval) Division and a London Territorial Division moved on north of the BELLEVUE RIDGE. The French bridged the ST. JANSBEEK, preparatory to clearing the swamps called the MERCKEM peninsula, which they and the Belgians cleared two days later. This threatened the Germans still entrenched in HOUTHULST FOREST.

On the 30th. October began the great final push for PASSCHENDAELE, which was to cover the Canadians with glory. At 5.50 a.m. in a cold clear dawn one battalion of the Canadian Mounted Rifles moved on rapidly. On their right were the 49th. and the Princess Patricias, which being the centre of the line suffered heavily, and further on three battalions of the 12th. Brigade. The latter captured Crest Farm in less than an hour from starting.

To the left of the Canadians was a British battalion — the Artists' Rifles, who met with such opposition that they, like the 49th., could advance scarce more than 150 yards. Nevertheless, in spite of this exposure of their flanks the C.M.R's kept on and after a hard day's fighting the troops found themselves entrenched at last on the outskirts of PASSCHEN-DAELE village. They had marched less than a mile, but every inch of the ground had been disputed, and the losses were heavy. No fewer than five strong counter-attacks were beaten off, our troops being greatly helped by the fire of captured machine-guns at CREST FARM.

The sodden state of the ground prevented the Artillery and the Naval Division from coming up, and the Canadian front formed a sharp Salient.

Next day under a tornado of German shelling the line went forward, the fighting concentrating about the pill-boxes.

" Black mud and great columns of debris were constantly being flung into the air. The soldiers at first cursed the mud, but after a time they had reason to bless it ; for the deep mud prevented innumerable German shells from burst-ing and saved thousands of lives ".

A few days of brighter weather followed, during which small advances were made and attacks repulsed, and then on November 6th. the Canadians struck another hammer-blow. The 3rd. and 4th. Divisions had meanwhile been replaced by the 1st. and 2nd. Divisions. The Germans had brought up large reinforcements, but although the Canadians fought in a salient, yet they had the advantage of high ground. The 27th. battalion swept through the village, of PASSCHEN-DAELE and beyond to the cross-roads. The hardest fight-ing took place at Vine Cottage and on the Goudberg Spur at Mosselmarkt stronghold, the entire garrison was either killed or captured. A hostile attack during the morning was beaten off and after losing 14.000 of their best and bravest, the men from the west could now from the top of the famous PASSCHENDAELE ridge survey at last the spires of ROULERS, MOORSLEDE and MENIN.

On Nov. 10th. British and Canadian troops attacked northwards from PASSCHENDAELE and GOUDBERG gaining after heavy fighting further ground on the main ridge.

It had been hoped at General Headquarters that the taking of Passchendaele would be the beginning of the end, and that now the Germans would evacuate northern Belgium. Our captures in Flanders since the end of July totalled 24.065 prisoners, 74 guns, 941 machine guns and 138 trench mortars. But alas, the fruits of victory could not be reaped. German troops and guns were pouring into the West from Russia, which had lamentably disappointed the hopes reposed in her. With forty fresh enemy divisions now to face, the winter on the British front and in the Ypres Salient appeared a gloomy prospect.

Nevertheless, the winter was endured and scarce was over than the enemy on the 21st March 1918, made their desperate spring which overthrew for a brief space all our defences. This was accompanied by a furious bombardment night and day. PASSCHENDAELE was given up. The Salient grew smaller daily ; yet the British divisions fought grimly on.

On April 26th. KEMMEL fell, and POPERINGHE was gradually evacuated of the civilian population. But no thought of leaving YPRES entered the head of the army commander. A day soon came when the defeat of the Germans in the great battle of AMIENS rendered its safety assured and made possible the triumphant march of the Allied Armies to the Rhine.

On October 14th. 1918 His Majesty King Albert, who had been given the command of all the Allied troops in Belgium ordered an attack on the whole front between DIXMUDE and COMINES. The British 2nd. Army of the veteran

General Plumer, was on the right and of this army the X.
and XIX. Corps pressed on for the last time through the
tragic Ypres Salient to the Summit of the ridge overlooking
MENIN and WERVICQ.   At the same time the II. Corps
advanced and captured MOORSEELE ; the French approached ROULERS and the Belgians entered ISEGHEM and
CORTEMARCK.   On the 16th. MENIN and WERVICQ
were captured and the road made clear for the relief of
LILLE, which on the following day (17th October 1918) was
entered by a British patrol to the great joy of the inhabitants.

The YPRES SALIENT, freed at last from the enemy, its
villages destroyed, its soil scarred and blighted, the trench
lines obliterated, belongs henceforward to history and will
for evermore be a sacred place for pilgrims to the graves of
the heroic dead.

———————

7

Lightning Source UK Ltd.
Milton Keynes UK
UKHW041843240522
403444UK00001B/64